University of Winnipeg, 515 Portage Ave., Winnipeg, MB. R3B 2E9 Canada

THE MONEY SUPPLY PROCESS

The Money Supply Process

A COMPARATIVE ANALYSIS

Dimitrije Dimitrijevic
and George Macesich

New York
Westport, Connecticut
London

Library of Congress Cataloging-in-Publication Data

Dimitrijević, Dimitrije.
    The money supply process : a comparative analysis / Dimitrije
Dimitrijević and George Macesich.
       p. cm.
    Includes bibliographical references and index.
    ISBN 0-275-93597-3
    1. Money supply. 2. Money supply—Mathematical models.
I. Macesich, George, 1927- . II. Title.
HG226.3.D56 1991
332.4'14—dc20   90-39155

Library of Congress Catalog Card Number: 90-39155
ISBN: 0-275-93597-3

First published in 1991

Praeger Publishers, One Madison Avenue, New York, NY 10010
An imprint of Greenwood Publishing Group, Inc.

Printed in the United States of America

∞™

The paper used in this book complies with the Permanent
Paper Standard issued by the National Information Standards
Organization (Z39.48—1984).

10 9 8 7 6 5 4 3 2 1

Contents

Tables

Preface

This book serves to commemorate the 30th anniversary of the Center for Yugoslav-American Studies, Research, and Exchanges at the Florida State University and its programs in comparative policy studies. It is an addition to a growing list of studies undertaken by the Center. These include such recent studies as *Essays on the Political Economy of Yugoslavia since 1974* (Rikard Lang, George Macesich, and Dragomir Vojnic, eds., 1982); *Money and Finance in Yugoslavia: A Comparative Analysis* (Dimitrije Dimitrijevic and George Macesich, 1984); *Essays on Comparative Managerial Practices in the U.S. and Yugoslavia* (Dan Voich and Mijat Damjanovic, eds., 1985); *Direct Foreign Investment in Yugoslavia: A Microeconomic Model* (T. Misha Sarkovic, 1986); *Dictionary of Yugoslav Political and Economic Terminology* [English/Serbo-Croatian] (Vlasta Andrlic and Ljiljana Jovkovic, eds., 1985); *Essays on the Yugoslav Economic Model* (George Macesich, Rikard Lang, and Dragomir Vojnic, eds., 1989).

The present volume deals with the money supply process (MSP), which represents one of the most complex and important topics of both monetary theory and monetary practice. This topic draws the interest of a broad group of economists involved in monetary and other financial matters, those working outside these fields, and noneconomists who usually consider the creation of money to be one of the most significant sources of economic disturbance. From the point of view of monetary and economic theory, MSP represents a significant part of the portfolio selection and wealth structure and behavior optimalization within the broad framework of wealth in economic theories. In monetary practice, it is not only the main target of monetary policy but also one of the most important instruments of economic policy.

An outstanding and complex characteristic of the MSP is its highly relative nature, which contributes to wide differences in the MSP in different types of economies. As a result, both theoretical and practical investigation of MSP requires a comparative analysis of this process to explain the differences that do occur in the MSP in these economies and what causes them. The relative nature of the MSP lends itself to a comparative study in order to properly define its general theory and overall monetary theory. This approach contributes to a better understanding of national MSP and offers a broad framework of possibilities for improving the efficiency of monetary policy in regulating the quantity of money. Indeed, the contributions of a comparative analysis of the MSP to a more general theory of the MSP, monetary theory, and financial theory create a better understanding of the differences in national MSP leading to the proper function of international financial organizations, especially in a better adjustment to the "conditionality" structure and other financial organizations involved in international financing and financial operations with different types of economies. Since financial money, instead of classic commodity money, is the only money used today, a comparative analysis of the MSP appears to be needed because of the increasing differentiation of the economies and their growing economic interdependence, particularly in international financing.

For comparative study, the MSP is defined here in much broader terms than is normally found in a standard analysis of the MSP in national economies that (1) mainly analyze the MSP in capitalist economies at the highest level of economic development; and (2) focus on the most differentiated financial and foreign exchange markets that undermine the MSP in socialist economies and those functioning on a lower economic development level. In a broader sense, comparative analysis of the MSP in this book is based on "wealth-approach" economic theories involving a more differentiated structure of variables and their relationships than is usual in recent national studies of the MSP:

—MSP is interpreted as part of the big picture in the monetary process, especially as it relates to demand for money and other financial instruments as counterparts to the demand for money, with the MSP acting as part of the monetary equilibrium process. In this way, not only monetary variables but nonmonetary financial variables and nonfinancial variables (domestic and foreign) have to be respected in this study of the MSP.

—Three different groups of agents influencing the MSP are the central banking system (monetary authorities), the other monetary institutions, and nonmonetary units (domestic and foreign).

—A differentiation of variables and their relationships in this study is based on their ability to be controlled in three groups: controllable, autonomous, and semicontrollable.

—The differences in the nature of the variables and the initial phase involving the creation/withdrawal of reserve money by the central banking system would be distinguished from the second phase, the process of monetary multiplication. As a result, within the monetary multiplication process, two types of variables and ratios emerge as "entropy" variables and ratios related to "degeneration" of reserve money and money in circulation, and "leakage" variables and ratios indicating outflow of money from the MSP.

Defined as a planetary comparative study, the classification of economies is of utmost importance. For empirical analysis possibilities, all economies involved are classified in two dimensions: basic types of institutional economic systems and economic development levels in a two-dimensional matrix presentation.

This analysis of the MSP requires an appropriate methodological approach based on a two-dimensional flow of funds accounts matrix, the most suitable for this complex, comparative analysis of the MSP. Consequently, the method of analysis and the empirical evidence for it are based on a flow-of-funds accounts matrix (stock and flow) that has been prepared for each economy included in this analysis. These accounts have been prepared for publication using the appropriate methodological approach by the Research Center of the National Bank of Yugoslavia and applying statistical information presented in country pages of the *International Financial Statistics*, The International Monetary Fund. However, these accounts also deserve attention as a basis for other comparative financial analyses. If this book stimulates their use for this purpose, then this study will have made a much needed contribution to a broader development of comparative financial studies by stimulating greater interest, awareness, and application of the treasure trove of comparative statistical information published by the International Monetary Fund in *International Financial Statistics* and other relevant publications.

This comparative, empirical study of the MSP uses the above statistical evidence, which involves around 50 variables and ratios for each of the one hundred countries involved from 1978 to 1983 and a dynamic analysis from 1979 to 1983, which includes about 15,000 variables and ratios. It is the first global comparative study of the MSP and money and finance that involves all of the basic types of economies and institutional economic systems at all levels of economic development. Thus defined, this planetary comparative study of the MSP is a pioneering work in comparative monetary and financial studies, necessarily involving the need for theoretical and methodological innovations that subsequent investigations are logically expected to improve.

The comparative study of the MSP is presented in six chapters. Chapter 1 presents the approach to an analysis of the MSP suitable for its use in a comparative analysis of the MSP while chapter 2 explains the concept and model of this analysis. Chapter 3 is designed to explain the classification of economies consistent with the concept and model of comparative analysis of the MSP. Chapter 4 explains the methodology applied in preparing the flow of funds accounts in this analysis and the statistical information used as presented in the *International Financial Statistics*, The International Monetary Fund. Chapters 5 through 8 show the empirical evidence and results of an empirical analysis of the MSP. Chapters 9 and 10 reveal the impact of balance of payments and institutional sectors on the MSP. Finally, chapter ll presents the summary of conclusions.

We are indeed indebted to Mrs. Esther C. S. Glenn, editor, Center for Yugoslav-American Studies, Research, and Exchanges, The Florida State University, for her editorial services.

THE MONEY SUPPLY PROCESS

1

Analysis of the Money Supply
Process in National Economies

The significant characteristic of traditional models for money supply process (MSP) analysis, especially relevant for a comparative analysis of the MSP, is their basic adjustment to the MSP in economies at the highest level of economic development. These economies have a highly differentiated financial structure, with convertible currency for world payments. Although very sophisticated, these analysis models for the MSP appear applicable in relatively few economies. They have little application in a large number of economies at the lower level of economic development that are burdened by a poorly differentiated financial structure and by currency that is either nonconvertible or hardly acceptable in foreign payments.

At least two deficiencies appear in a comparative analysis of the process in traditional analysis models for the MSP:

1. They neglect the impact of foreign exchange transactions (foreign assets and liabilities) of monetary institutions on the MSP that are very significant in economies at the lower level of economic development, with a low differentiation of financial institutions, financial instruments, and currency that cannot be used for foreign payments.

2. They disregard the possibility of holding significant monetary and nonmonetary deposits with the central banking system for nonmonetary units. This has been observed in many economies, particularly socialist economies with centralized economic decisionmaking, at the lower level of economic development with lower degrees of differentiation of monetary and financial organization.

This chapter will present an analysis model for the MSP in a national economy that eliminates the deficiencies found in a traditional analysis as a basis to define the concept and model for a comparative analysis of the MSP. This will be presented in chapter 2. The monetary analysis concept and the role of analysis in the MSP are explained first, followed by a presentation of the analysis model for the MSP in national economies that could be used in a comparative analysis of the MSP.

MONETARY ANALYSIS AND ANALYSIS OF THE MSP

Broadly speaking, monetary analysis may be defined as the analysis of changes in the quantity of money and the result of the ramifications of these changes on economic developments (financial and nonfinancial), especially as they influence price development, production, exports, and imports. However, this apparently simple concept of monetary analysis involves complex questions related to changes in the money supply and demand for money. Four important groups of questions emerge: (1) the definition of money supply and other monetary aggregates; (2) the process of creating a money supply and other monetary aggregates; (3) the demand for money and other monetary aggregates; (4) the monetary equilibrium process involving the results of monetary instability and the elimination of the discrepancy between supply and demand for money.

Thus, monetary analysis is supposed to answer these questions: Which financial instruments are to be considered money? Are several definitions of monetary aggregates (M_1, M_2) to be used in monetary policy and economic development analysis? What changes occurred in monetary aggregates and what causes and transactions contributed to these changes? How have the changes in demand for money compared with changes in money supply? Is the demand for monetary aggregates equal to, less than, or greater than the quantity of these aggregates? Do these monetary aggregate developments and demand for these aggregates mean monetary equilibrium or disequilibrium? What adjustment processes and results have been observed in monetary disequilibrium? A monetary analysis is expected to answer these questions and to make possible predictions of future developments.

These are clearly theoretical questions making the fine line between monetary and financial and economic analysis rather vague. This ambiguity occurs again in the line between the creation-of-money analysis and monetary analysis:

1. Monetary analysis may define money supply in different ways, beginning with the definition of instruments of direct payment and high

degree of liquidity not used as direct payment instruments, which have a similar influence on the behavior of their holders. Thus, Milton Friedman suggests that the definition of money should include the structure of liquid instruments that results in the most stable parameters in empirical monetary equations. In this way, the definition of money supply may include a differentiated structure of financial instruments that may be the subject of both monetary and financial analysis. This makes the border between monetary and financial analysis rather relative, depending on the intent and type of monetary analysis. The other money supply source occurs in the differences in the determinants and the effects of holding money by the different institutional sectors; this creates a different definition of money for the individual institutional sectors. Therefore, using one definition for the whole economy is really a simplification of money supply definition problems. The practical solution is that money supply in the narrow sense (M_1), including instruments of direct payment, is used as the first aggregate, and broader definitions are used according to the purpose of the monetary analysis.

2. Analysis of the MSP is obviously dependent on the definition of monetary aggregate. Consequently, the model and methodology of analysis of the MSP involves all of these ambiguities related to aggregate definition. In addition, the purpose of monetary analysis may involve direct or indirect influences on changes in monetary aggregates—here again, the borderline between monetary and financial analysis is rather vague. The analysis of the MSP does not appear to be very clearly defined in monetary or financial analysis.

3. The estimate of demand for money represents one of the most difficult monetary analysis problems in the realm of development expectations. Thus, the demand function of money first depends on the definition of money. Then, it becomes logically related to demand functions for other financial and nonfinancial assets.[1] In this way, monetary analysis has to involve utility preference behavior—that is, within the optimal portfolio of choice decisionmaking, with the demand for money included in the decisionmaking process by the individual units. The application of this approach to an analysis of the demand for money obviously leads to a wide range of monetary and financial analysis topics, making the boundary between the two unclear.

4. Analysis of the monetary disequilibrium process involves broad monetary transactions (other than financial and nonfinancial) leading to the elimination of monetary disequilibrium. These set in motion changes in (1) the demand for money based on increase or decrease in production and prices; (2) stocks of liquid financial instruments; (3) interest rates;

(4) money supply, because of an increase or decrease in exports and imports and foreign exchange transactions by monetary institutions; and (5) transfer of money into nonmonetary financial instruments.

This results in an analysis of the MSP that can be defined as a consistent, causally interrelated part of monetary analysis broadly related to financial analysis and nonfinancial transactions as well.

There should be some clarification of the relationship of monetary analysis and MSP analysis to monetary theory and monetary policy. Monetary analysis and monetary theory investigate the same set of topics, but the purpose of each is different: monetary theory investigates the laws governing monetary developments while monetary analysis is expected to explain the actual developments for the practical needs of monetary policy. Thus, monetary analysis, including analysis of the MSP, uses monetary theory to (1) investigate actual developments, (2) forecast monetary planning needs, and (3) decide monetary policy measures for the implementation of planned monetary policy targets. However, the reverse relationship is also significant because empirical findings in monetary analysis may contribute new ideas to the progress of monetary theory, serving as an instrument to test the theoretical hypothesis.

THE ANALYSIS MODEL FOR THE MSP IN NATIONAL ECONOMIES

The analysis model for the MSP in national economies is designed to serve as a construction model for a comparative analysis of the MSP. Since the national economies interpretation for the MSP model is adjusted to the comparative analysis needs of the MSP, this analysis model for the MSP in decentralized economic decisionmaking economies with decentralized monetary and financial organizations should be used as the basic model. Therefore, it is not difficult to adjust it to analyze the MSP of economies with lower degrees of decentralized economic decisionmaking and decentralized monetary and financial organizations. Also, this model lends itself well to an analysis of the MSP in economies at different levels of economic development. In addition, it assumes there is a significant differentiation between financial institutions and financial instruments in both domestic and foreign financial instruments, which are related to creation/withdrawal of reserve money and monetary multiplication. As a result, both stock and flow concepts of the MSP have to be applied; the stock concept presents the relationships at the beginning and end, while the flow concept explains the changes in relationships in the MSP in the time frame under consideration.

After this approach, an explanation of the analysis model of the MSP involves a presentation of the theoretical hypothesis of the MSP followed by an explanation of the significant transactions, relationships, and role of different types of agents in the MSP. This defines the comparative analysis model of the MSP in national economies.

The Theoretical Hypothesis of the MSP

The MSP may be included within the broad framework of economic decisionmaking, which is designed to reach the optimal utility combination of monetary, financial, and nonfinancial assets that would yield the maximum return on assets with minimal risk, within the existing budget constraints. In a narrow sense, the MSP could be explained as part of the monetary equilibrium process.

Broadly speaking, the MSP is part of three groups of causally interrelated transactions:

1. Real transactions that determine relationships with monetary and other financial transactions as reflected in financial surpluses and financial deficits of the individual economic units or institutional sectors;
2. Financial intermediation that transfers financial surpluses to economic units having financial deficits; and
3. Financial transactions that cause domestic and foreign changes in monetary aggregates performed by monetary and nonmonetary units.

With the MSP as a part of the monetary equilibrium process, it represents the initial cause of monetary imbalance and is part of the process to eliminate it. There are two kinds of monetary imbalance—in the supply/demand on reserve money by monetary institutions and in supply/demand on money in circulation. In a reserve money imbalance, other monetary institutions react by increasing or decreasing their investment. This leads to the elimination of extra reserve money or a shortage of reserve money in the accounts of these monetary institutions within the central banking system.

The elimination of imbalance in the supply/demand on money in circulation goes hand in hand with this process of eliminating the imbalance in supply/demand on reserve money. Thus, creation of more reserve money than there is demand for it leads to an extra increase in bank credits, which causes an extra increase in the money supply. This process initiates an increase in demand for goods and services and nonmonetary financial instruments. These developments lead to an increase in production and prices, thereby contributing to an increase in the demand for money. However, one effect of monetary imbalance is the deterioration of balance-of-payments and foreign financial transactions of monetary institutions, resulting in a withdrawal of the money supply. In addition, it affects financial investments in nonmonetary instruments as a short-term consideration or decreased money supply.

Within this framework, transactions involved in the MSP should be classified in two groups: (1) transactions of creation (withdrawal) of reserve money performed by the central banking system (monetary authorities); and (2) transactions representing the multiplication of reserve money by other monetary institutions. Thus, MSP can be presented by the following basic formula:

$$M = cA \cdot m \qquad\qquad (1)$$

where, as stocks and as flows (change in the stock),

M = money supply

cA = reserve money (primary money; high-powered money)

m = monetary multiplier, indicating the number of units of money supply created (withdrawn) as a result of one unit of creation (withdrawal) of reserve money

Reserve money (cA), both as stock and as flow (change in stock) amount, is defined as the sum of domestic investments of the central banking system or monetary authorities increased or decreased by the amount of net foreign assets of the central banking system.[2]

Monetary multiplication represents a far more complex part of the MSP.

At this stage in the explanation of the MSP, it is necessary to present the outcome of the MSP in the monetary equilibrium process. The first step in this process begins with the creation of extra reserve money, an extra holding of reserve money by other monetary institutions, which is followed by an increase in credits or other investments by the institutions to nonmonetary units. This means an increase in money supply followed by (1) more investments by nonmonetary units in nonmonetary financial instruments; and (2) additional buying of goods and services that could lead to a deterioration in the balance of payments and increase in foreign liabilities or decrease in foreign assets. In this way, the result of the monetary equilibrium process is a change in money supply (parallel with the appropriate change in demand for money) that may be presented by this equation:

$$M \;=\; A \;-\; T + E_n \qquad\qquad (2)$$

where (in stock or in flow terms)

M = money supply

A = total domestic financial investments of monetary institutions in credits and other instruments issued by domestic units

T = total financial investments of nonmonetary units in nonmonetary deposits and other instruments issued by monetary institutions

E_n = net foreign assets of monetary institutions (foreign assets, E_a, minus foreign liabilities, E_l)

Under the next heading, this equation 2 will be included in the formula for monetary multiplier to interpret the above monetary multiplication process. At the same time, this equation can be identified in the balance sheet of monetary institutions and in the monetary sector in flow-of-funds accounts. This connects the empirical analysis of the MSP with the other details in the balance sheets and flow-of-funds accounts.

The stock and flow concepts of the MSP used in this analysis are particularly important for a longer period, which involves the stock reserve money and the stock multiplier at the beginning and end. A simultaneous occurrence in this process involves the flow of reserve money creation and monetary multiplication. In a normal setting, these two components of the MSP in stock and flow concepts very often differ significantly. This is very important in monetary multipliers reflecting differences in both controlled and autonomous variables in monetary multiplication. As a result, the definition of these two concepts of the MSP needs clarification to facilitate an understanding of their differences, which is important for an MSP analysis in developing economies that undergo rapid changes in their economic structure and relationships relevant to the MSP in relatively short periods of time.

A summary of the process in the creation of money in the broad framework of all economic processes can be presented using the matrix of flow-of-funds accounts; this involves institutional sectors vertically and types of transactions/instruments horizontally. The process is assumed to start with reserve money disequilibrium (imbalance) in the sector of other monetary institutions, which were created by new issue of reserve money by the central banking system[3] or by a horizontal influence in the matrix of flow-of-funds account going from the central banking system to other monetary institutions. This unbalanced state in other monetary institutions initiates the appropriate increase in their investments. For instance, credits to nonmonetary units, which are a part of the portfolio selection decisionmaking process, are reflected vertically in this sector of the matrix of flow-of-funds account. At the same time, the matrix registers horizontally the countereffects of these investments in nonmonetary sectors as a new imbalance is created: these sectors hold back money, buy extra goods and services, or make financial investments, which are contributing factors to a new portfolio selection decision. In this way, the matrix of the flow-of-funds account presents all transactions in two dimensions: (1) part of the portfolio selection decisionmaking process in one institutional sector (vertically); and (2) a source for the creation of monetary imbalance in other institutional sectors (horizontally); this creates its own vertical portfolio selection that eliminates its monetary imbalance but does create a horizontal monetary imbalance in some other sector. In this process, monetary imbalance is forever decreasing through the increasing demand for money and diminishing money supply to reach a new monetary equilibrium.

Reserve Money

By definition, reserve money includes the total domestic investments of the central bank, including an increase from net foreign assets or decrease in the net foreign liabilities of the central banking system. On the balance sheet of the central banking system, reserve money is the total amount of assets minus the amount of foreign liabilities. Thus, it involves central bank credits to other monetary institutions in different forms of credits, including discounts, purchase of securities, domestic purchase and sale of foreign exchange, and foreign lending and borrowing.

As a counterpart of the assets side of reserve money, the liability side of the balance sheet for the central banking system shows the ways reserve money is held in (1) accounts of other monetary institutions, (2) accounts of the central government, and (3) accounts of other nonmonetary units in currency in circulation. A broader concept of reserve money is used in this analysis than normal for these funds, as money in accounts at other monetary institutions with the central banking system, plus the currency in circulation. A broad definition of reserve money gives a more suitable basis for a comparative analysis of the MSP, especially in a comparative analysis of the dual role of the central banking system to help create reserve money, as well as to regulate monetary multiplication.

By using mathematical symbols, the amount of reserve money in the central banking system can be presented in two ways: (1) in an equation presenting the structure of the assets side of the balance sheet, and (2) in an equation presenting the structure of the liabilities side of the balance sheet.

The reserve money equation based on the assets side of the balance sheet for the central banking system has this general form:

$$c_A = c_{Ad} + c_{En} \tag{3}$$
$$c_{Ad} = c_{Ag} + c_{An} + c_{Am} + c_{Ua} \tag{4}$$
$$c_{En} = c_{Ea} - c_{El} \tag{5}$$

where

c_A	=	creation of reserve money
c_{Ad}	=	creation of reserve money by domestic money transactions
c_{En}	=	creation of reserve money by foreign exchange transactions
c_{Ag}	=	forms of credits to the central government
c_{An}	=	forms of credits to other nonmonetary units
c_{Am}	=	forms of credits to other monetary institutions
c_{Ua}	=	other assets, unclassified
c_{Ea}	=	foreign assets
c_{El}	=	foreign liabilities

Thus, the classification of the assets side of reserve money creation is based on institutional sectors rather than on types of transactions. This classification is more suitable for a comparative analysis on the assumption that the presentation of the share of institutional sectors as beneficiaries of reserve money creation provides for a better indication of the nature of the creation process of this money and the basic differences this process undergoes in other economies. However, this presentation does not exclude a classification of the creation of reserve money by types of instruments or by the matrix presentation by institutional sectors and types of instruments.

The structure of reserve money on the liability side of the balance sheet of the central banking system may be presented by this equation:

$$c^A = R + C + {}_cDM + {}_cT \qquad (6)$$

where

R = balances on accounts of other monetary institutions with the central banking system

C = currency in circulation

${}_cDM$ = deposit money of nonmonetary domestic residents with the central banking system

${}_cT$ = nonmonetary liabilities of the central banking system to nonmonetary domestic residents

Reserve money in accounts of other monetary institutions (R) should be, if possible, disaggregated into three parts: (1) R_v, representing the amount of reserve money corresponding to the demand for reserve money by the other monetary institutions; (2) R_o, representing obligatory holding of reserve money in countries where this money is held on the same account as voluntary holding of reserve money (R_v); and (3) R_t, representing temporary holding of extra reserve money or a lower amount of that corresponding to demand for reserve money during monetary multiplication. This disaggregation of reserve money on accounts of other monetary institutions in the central banking system can provide useful information on the behavior of these institutions in the monetary multiplication process; however, its statistical identification is rather difficult.

Equations of reserve money based on the assets side of the central banking system balance sheet, equations 3, 4, and 5 are designed to explain reserve money creation based on the liabilities side of this balance sheet (equation 6), which can explain the monetary multiplication process.

Monetary Multiplier

Here we will explain the first variable ($_cA$) in the basic formula of the MSP (equation 1), followed by the more complex process of monetary multiplication, as presented by the monetary multiplier (m).

The monetary multiplication process is usually initiated by the creation of extra reserve money, which causes reserve money imbalance. This is followed by a series of subsequent investments of the extra reserve money by other monetary institutions (A). On one hand, it is accompanied by an increase in money supply (M), a transfer of one part of this money supply in nonmonetary financial instruments (T), and its influence on foreign exchange transactions of monetary institutions (E_n) contributing to changes in money supply. On the other hand, these developments cause an increase in the holding of currency in circulation (C), monetary ($_cDM$) and nonmonetary deposits ($_cT$) with the central banking system by nonmonetary units, and increased demand for holding reserve money in monetary institution accounts (R) with the central banking system. The first process leads to an increase in money supply, and the second process means elimination of extra reserve money. Both processes end when the extra reserve money disappears from the accounts of other monetary institutions with the central banking system (R) or when the balances on these accounts are equal to the demand for reserve money by other monetary institutions.

These two different processes in monetary multiplication may be presented by the formula

$$m \; = \; M{:}_cA \tag{7}$$

As we have explained,

$$M \; = \; A - T + E_n \tag{2}$$

and

$$_cA \; = \; R + C + {}_cDM + {}_cT \tag{6}$$

so that:

$$M = (A - T + E_n) : (R + C + {_c}DM + {_c}T) \quad (8)$$

The numerator of this formula explains the creation of the money supply process; it changes as a result of investments of monetary institutions (A), investments of money in nonmonetary investments by nonmonetary units (T), and foreign exchange transactions of monetary institutions (E_n); and the denominator presents the use of reserve money. Both groups of variables are observed in the monetary multiplication process.

The characteristics of the monetary multiplier formula have to be explained for a better understanding of the monetary multiplication process and its presentation by monetary multipliers.

First, the monetary multiplier formula (equation 8) in the numerator includes the variable related to foreign exchange transactions of monetary institutions (E_n), but there is no variable presenting these transactions in the denominator involving the liability side of the central banking system. The question may be: If E_n includes net foreign assets (stock or changes) of all monetary institutions, including those of the central banking system, why is there no appropriate variable in the denominator? It was shown that this variable ($_cE_n$) is considered a part of the assets side of the reserve money (equation 3). The logic of this is that $_cE_n$ is considered to be the result of the central bank's other monetary institutions—foreign transactions in addition to central bank—foreign resident transactions, foreign lending and borrowing. Thus, $_cE_n$ is not included in the monetary multiplication process in the same way as E_n, representing the result of foreign exchange transactions of other monetary institutions with non-monetary domestic units. Then, the variable $_cE_n$ can be fully controlled by the central banking system in the same way other instruments of reserve money creation are controlled by this system. The mechanism of change in both of these variables ($_cE_n$, E_n) is explained later in this section.

Second, the monetary multiplier formula (equation 8), involving absolute amounts of variables, is not suitable for an understanding of the relevant relationships, especially in comparative analysis, and must be transformed by a formula with ratios of variables. A workable solution may be to present these variables by their ratios to total investments of monetary institutions (A). The reasoning behind this solution is that these investments (A) are basic to the monetary multiplication process: Reserve money ($_cA$) influences investments of other monetary institutions (A) that increases the money supply (M). This increased money supply influences nonmonetary investments (T), foreign exchange transactions resulting in changes in money, and changes in the reserve money structure presented in the denominator of equation 8. In this way, variable A presents the variable in both numerator and denominator of equation 8 as ratios of A, noting the relationships in the monetary multiplication process. Accordingly, the monetary multiplier (m) is

$$
\begin{aligned}
m &= (1 - t + f) : (e + c + d + ct) = k{:}p \qquad (9) \\
k &= 1 - t + f \\
p &= e + c + d + ct \\
t &= T{:}A \\
f &= E_n{:}A \\
e &= R{:}A \\
c &= C{:}A \\
d &= {}_cDM{:}A \\
ct &= {}_cT{:}A
\end{aligned}
$$

The Role of the Time Variable

Equations 7 and 8 do not involve the time variable, which may appear strange since the monetary multiplication process includes the time variable. The effects of multiplication are greater over a longer period of time, including successive investments of extra reserve money—up to the final elimination of extra reserve money (by entropy and leakage) from the monetary multiplication process. As a result, the monetary multiplier strongly depends on the time variable, although the theoretical conclusion is difficult to put into practice. Reserve money is created every day in practical experience and in different amounts, which makes identification of individual multiplication processes very difficult in the individual creation of reserve money.

In practice, the existence of some extra reserve money or its shortage in restrictive monetary policy should be assumed, or that the monetary multiplication process, which began some time ago by creating extra reserve money, has been ended or that reserve money has been inherited and transferred in an extra amount from one period to the next. The best solution is to assume there is no extra reserve money or that the inherited extra reserve money is transferred to the next period; this means that the monetary multiplication process is ended. In mathematical terms, it is assumed that the time period included in the formula of the monetary multiplier is infinite or long enough for all extra money to be absorbed by entropy and leakage.[4] If this assumption is unacceptable, the results must be considered in interpreting the evidence. The danger of mistakes with this assumption is in (1) the significant fluctuation in the creation of reserve money; and (2) the cessation of a further increase in reserve money and its withdrawal. In a short period, it is possible to have monetary multiplication that deviates very significantly from expectations based on the assumption of zero inherited extra reserve money or the shortage of reserve money.

Classification of Variables and Their Ratios

An explanation of the variables involved in equations 7 and 8 will reveal a different nature and role in the monetary multiplication process that should lead to a better understanding of this process.

The basic classification of variables and their ratios in monetary multiplication is observable in equations 2 and 6 that present two different groups of these variables and their ratios in the numerator and the other in the denominator of the multiplier equations 7, 8, and 9. As indicated, the variables and ratios in the numerator explain the role of credits of monetary institutions (A), the investments of money in nonmonetary financial instruments (T), and foreign exchange transactions (E_n) in the monetary multiplication process arising from a portfolio selection of monetary and nonmonetary units and the influence of balance-of-payments transactions. Variables and ratios presented in the denominator of these equations involve that part of the reserve money structure that influences monetary multiplication. Both groups involve variables and ratios, as well as those reflecting autonomous decisionmaking by other monetary institutions and nonmonetary units (domestic and foreign) that are controlled by the central banking system.

Another factor in the classification of these variables and ratios appears to be their specific character and influence on monetary multiplication. In this respect, the variables and ratios in equations 8 and 9 may be classified into three groups: variables representing the creation of money, variables and ratios representing leakage of money or outflow of money and reserve money from the monetary multiplication process, and variables and ratios representing entropy of reserve money.

The concept of entropy in thermodynamics, the second law of thermodynamics, expresses degradation of heat energy induced in a closed system by its dissipation into latent energy or heating the system. This concept was first used by Nicholas Georgescu-Roegen in other sciences, including economic science[5]; it will reveal the role of some variables in the MSP that represents the degradation of their position. In the monetary multiplication process, it should be used for degradation of reserve money by its transformation into latent reserve money, which has been eliminated from the monetary multiplication process. The term entropy in the MSP involves the demand for money or the quantity of money corresponding to the demand for money. This means transforming a part of the money supply into latent money that has been eliminated from the monetary equilibrium process or from the quantity of money influencing financial and nonfinancial transactions. Defined in this way, entropy of reserve money and money supply are obviously different from the leakage of money and reserve money that are influenced by different factors with results relevant to the monetary processes for monetary multiplication.

According to these criteria, the variables and ratios in equations 7, 8, and 9 should be classified in the following groups:

— Variable representing the creation of money: A;
— Variables and ratios meaning leakage of money and reserve money; and
— Entropy of reserve money: R, e.

This classification explains the basic nature of these variables and ratios. However, it is possible that they may have an opposite effect, as with a decrease in T, withdrawal of money by foreign exchange transactions, and decrease in currency in circulation, C.

The third classification relates to the institutional sectors and control over them. The most significant one, which is responsible for control over the monetary multiplication process, is the central banking sector or the monetary authorities sector. The main variable controlled by it is reserve money on accounts of other monetary institutions (R) through the obligatory reserve ratio. However, this control is related only to the minimal amount of this reserve money. In other economies, regulations imposing obligatory holding of some restricted deposits or deposit money with the central banking system are used. In these cases, variables $_cT$ and $_cDM$ may also be classified as controlled ($_cT$) or absorbed ($_cDM$) by the central banking system. The other monetary institutions mainly control the amount of the reserve money account with the central banking system beyond the obligatory reserve (R,e), which is related to the control of bank investment amounts (A). The leakage of money (T, E_n, t, f) mainly depends on decisionmaking by nonmonetary units. The same is valid for the leakage of reserve money into currency in circulation (C,c).

With the influence of institutional sectors on the MSP, the macroeconomic motivation and behavior of the central banking system should be distinguished from microeconomic motivation and behavior of other institutional sectors.

The next classification of variables and ratios involved in monetary multiplication relates to the generality of these variables and ratios, which are aimed at facilitating their use in an analysis of the monetary multiplication process. The most general ratios are the "complex" ratios k and p. Ratio k presents ratios in the numerator on the right side of equation 9 showing the effects of the creation of money by monetary institutions (A) and the leakage of money (T, E_n):

$$k = 1 - t + f \tag{10}$$

Ratio p presents ratios in the denominator on the right side of equation 9 or ratios explaining use of reserve money by monetary and nonmonetary entities—entropy of reserve money (e) and leakage of reserve money (c, d, ct):

$$p = e + d + ct \tag{11}$$

so that the monetary multiplier is

$$m = k{:}p$$

as shown in equation 9.

The second level of generality includes basic variables and basic ratios involving variables/ratios presented on the right side of equations 8 and 9 in the numerator and the denominator.

Finally, a subclassification of basic ratios into explanatory ratios is designed for a more detailed explanation of the basic ratios in the extra changes and size of these ratios. This subclassification of basic variables will depend on the nature of these ratios in individual economies and the differences in size and in the variability of these explanatory ratios, which contribute to the extraordinary size and variations in the basic ratios. This basic ratio subclassification may be particularly useful for a better understanding of controllability and autonomous forces affecting multiplication and the whole MSP.

Submultipliers and Reciprocal Multipliers

Presentation of the monetary multiplier resulting from submultipliers may also contribute to a better understanding of the monetary multiplication process. Thus, a monetary multiplier (m) can be presented as the sum of three submultipliers:

$$m \;=\; m_a - m_t + m_f \qquad\qquad (12)$$

where

$$m_a \;=\; A{:}_cA \;\text{(credit multiplier)} \qquad\qquad (13)$$
$$m_t \;=\; T{:}_cA \;\text{(nonmonetary liabilities multiplier)} \qquad\qquad (14)$$
$$m_f \;=\; E_n{:}_cA \;\text{(foreign transactions multiplier)} \qquad\qquad (15)$$

These submultipliers may prove particularly significant if they are more stable than the basic ratios as a basis for monetary planning.

In addition to the above monetary multipliers, similar arguments may lead to the conclusion that reciprocal multipliers should be consulted as well. Defined as a ratio of the number of units of reserve money per one unit of money supply, this multiplier is

$$m_r \;=\; {}_cA{:}M \qquad\qquad (16)$$

and

$$M_r \;=\; (R + C + {}_cDM + {}_cT){:}M \qquad\qquad (17)$$

or

$$m_r \;=\; R{:}M + C{:}M + {}_cDM{:}M + {}_cT{:}M \qquad\qquad (18)$$

The use of these multipliers and relevant ratios will depend on their contribution to a better understanding of the role of individual variables in the monetary multiplication process, especially if they are more stable than the regular multipliers.

Among these submultipliers, the most significant would appear to be the credit multiplier, which may be defined in comparison with the monetary multiplier. According to the credit multiplier equation (equation 13) and equation 2, a credit multiplier can be presented by

$$m_a = (M + T - E_n):cA \qquad (19)$$

or

$$m_a = m + T:E_n-cA = m + t:p - f:p$$

so that finally

$$m_a = 1:p \qquad (20)$$

Thus, while the monetary multiplier depends on two complex ratios—ratio k (leakage of money) and ratio p (leakage and entropy of reserve money)—the credit multiplier depends only on the complex ratio p (leakage and entropy of reserve money). In other words, the credit multiplier explains the creation of money by monetary institutions, excluding leakage of money created in this way (T, E_n). However, if the next explanation of the interrelationships between the creation of money by monetary institutions (A) and the leakage of money (T, E_n) is considered, the variables T and E_n have an indirect if not a direct effect on the credit multiplier.

An analysis of the role that entropy and leakage of reserve money (ratio p) play in the MSP, considering the monetary multiplier, can be used to analyze the credit multiplier.

Significant Interrelationships among Variables

The variables and ratios involved in equations 8 and 9 are presented as separate determinants in monetary multiplication. However, significant relationships among them influence the size of the ratios and monetary multipliers.

The significant relationships relate to investments of monetary institutions (A) and leakage of money in nonmonetary liabilities of these institutions (T). The relatively greater T leads to a relatively greater A, which increases the credit capacity of the monetary institutions. However, the greater A, the lower ratios are in equation 9. Thus, it may happen that the higher or lower ratios in this equation in a comparison over a period of time or with other economies are the result of a relatively greater or lower T; this produces a negligible influence on the monetary multiplier (m).

Another factor is the relationship between monetary institution investments (A) and the monetary effects of foreign exchange transactions by monetary institutions (E_n) that may contribute to relatively higher or lower ratios in equation 9. The simultaneous creation or leakage of money by foreign exchange transactions means an absorption or increase in the credit capacity of monetary institutions resulting in higher payments for foreign exchange from domestic residents, with the opposite being true as well. In this way, unlike leakage of money to nonmonetary liabilities of monetary institutions (T), the creation of money by foreign exchange transactions or by monetary institutions (E_n) leads to lower investments by these institutions, with relatively higher ratios in equation 9, which must be considered when comparing these ratios in a time frame among economies with the opposite scenario in leakage of money by foreign exchange transactions.

The share of currency in circulation (C) in total money supply (M) or the currency in circulation to deposit money (DM) ratio may significantly influence the size of the monetary multiplier: the greater this ratio, the lower the monetary multiplier, with the opposite being true in a lower $C:DM$ ratio.

Stock and Flow (Static and Dynamic) Multipliers

The MSP can be interpreted in a static and dynamic approach. In the same way, monetary multiplication and monetary multipliers can be interpreted as stock and flow relationships within this approach to the MSP.

The stock monetary multiplier reflects relationships of stock variables observable at the beginning or end of a period. Thus, it reflects the financial instrument structure related to the behavior of the portfolio selection of economic units that have been adjusted to the motives influencing this behavior. This involves the influences of current economic measures and developments, such as interest and exchange rates, risk of losses, expectations of price developments, and influences related to the structure of the economic system and level of economic development—an important factor in comparative analysis. In this way, the stock monetary multiplier reflects the structure of the demand for money and other financial instruments relevant to monetary multiplication.

The flow multiplier reflects changes in the stocks of relevant financial instruments in this study. If a stock multiplier has been changed during this period, the flow monetary multiplier explains how this change has been performed and which variables and ratios have contributed to the changes in the monetary multiplier from the beginning to the end. It is obvious that differences between stock and flow multipliers have to be greater than changes in the stock multipliers; and greater changes in variables and their ratios involved in flow multipliers are to be assumed.

Stock and flow monetary multipliers have different economic meanings. The stock monetary multiplier reflects the behavior of economic subjects seeking to optimize the level and structure of their real and financial assets (monetary and nonmonetary) into what they suppose is the optimal combination of maximal profit and security. This reflects the decisions of economic subjects as to which part of their current income to consume and which part to invest in real and/or financial assets, and within financial assets, which part to hold in the form of money to reach this optimal combination of profit and security. The flow monetary multiplier on the other hand indicates the transactions of economic units within a period of time to reach this optimal combination of profit and security of assets, and the corresponding stock monetary multipliers.

Therefore, a combined analysis of the static and flow monetary multipliers may be expected to provide the optimal results for an analysis of monetary multipliers. This is particularly relevant for economic development causing changes in economic growth pertinent to the MSP. A dramatic change in the foreign market would also affect financial and nonfinancial domestic economic development to impose extraordinary economic and monetary policy measures, causing changes in the MSP.

The Nature of the Monetary Multiplier

It is necessary to explain the nature of the monetary multiplier in order to avoid oversimplification that could lead to a misinterpretation of its size, sign, and changes. Four cases are explained: $m > 1$, $0 < m < 1$, $m < 0$, and $m = 0$.

A monetary multiplier greater than 1.0 is the normal case that fully corresponds to the definition of monetary multiplication. There may be two varieties here: both M and $_cA$ are positive, and both M and $_cA$ are negative. In the first case, the creation of reserve money ($_cA$) leads to the creation of a greater amount of money supply (M). In the second, the withdrawal of reserve money ($-_cA$) results in a withdrawal of money supply in a greater amount than the withdrawal of reserve money. As a result, both of the positive and negative processes of multiplication are expressed by a positive multiplier, which means the monetary multiplication process multiplies the impact of the creation of reserve money or the withdrawal of reserve money moving under the direction of the reserve money variable (cA). In this sense, the process of monetary multiplication does not change the influence of reserve money.

The second case is very close to the first case in the influence of reserve money (cA) on money supply. However, the difference is that the effect of the process of monetary multiplication on the money supply (M) is lower than the amount of reserve money creation. This appears contradictory to the concept of the multiplication of reserve money when a unit of reserve money is accompanied by less than one unit of money supply. This happens, first, in a large leakage of money (T, E_n) compared with the creation of money by bank investments (A), usually resulting from a relatively large demand for nonmonetary deposits. Second is the leakage of money by foreign exchange transactions of monetary institutions that led to a relative strong reduction in credit capacity and investments of monetary institutions. Third, the influence of reserve money creation on the creation of money by investments by monetary institutions (A) may be relatively low because of a larger entropy of reserve money (e) or because of a greater leakage of reserve money (c,d,ct), and other combinations leading to a lower increase or decrease in money supply than the increase or decrease in the amount of reserve money. The significant conclusion in this case is that monetary multiplication involves exogenous influences that may strengthen or weaken the effects of reserve money creation, which may be caused not only by the behavior of monetary institutions but by the domestic and foreign nonmonetary units.

The third case, negative monetary multipliers, appears more contradictory than the second. It involves a decrease in money supply $(M<0)$ in spite of the creation of reserve money $(cA>0)$, or increase in money supply $(M>0)$ in spite of a decrease in reserve money $(cA<0)$. These are the opposite effects of monetary multiplication in a narrow sense on one hand and the stronger exogenous influences on monetary multiplication on the other hand. If monetary multiplication in the narrow sense is assumed to be reflected in changes in the credit multiplier m_a (equation 13), the exogenous effects are primarily reflected in a nonmonetary liabilities multiplier m_t (equation 14) and foreign transactions multiplier m_f (equation 15). Under this assumption, it appears that the negative monetary multiplier reflecting positive cA and negative M may be explained as a result of greater leakage of money (E_n-T) than the creation of money by investments of monetary institutions (A) in equation 8. Or, in other words, the result of lower positive credit multiplier (m_a) than the negative sum of the other two multipliers $(m_f - m_t)$ in equation 12.

When a negative monetary multiplier is found as a result of a negative $_cA$ (withdrawal of reserve money) and a positive money supply (M), there is an overcompensation for the effects of reserve money withdrawal by the countereffects of lower leakage and entropy of reserve money ($C,_cDM,_cT:R$). This process has made possible an increase in investments of monetary institutions (A) possible in spite of a decrease in $_cA$, accompanied by a relatively lower leakage of money (E_n-T) than creation of money by investments of monetary institutions (A) in equation 8. This may be a result of some other combination of variables in equation 8 leading to a positive algebraic sum of the credit multiplier (m_a) and the other two multipliers in the numerator of equation 12. In this way, the basic characteristic of contrary development in reserve money creation on one hand, and money supply on the other, is a stronger countereffect of exogenous influences on monetary multiplication (on leakage and entropy of money supply and reserve money) than the effect of monetary multiplication in a narrow sense (reflected in the investments of monetary institutions).

Finally, the fourth case, portraying no reserve money creation ($_cA = 0$), cannot be considered monetary multiplication if there is no creation of reserve money or multiplication of it. However, the pure case of $_cA = 0$ is rather exceptional—usually, in practice, there is a rather low, positive or negative $_cA$, very close to zero. Because of the rather low $_cA$, even if there is a correspondingly moderate change in money supply, the result is an extraordinarily high monetary multiplier.

The wide differences in monetary multipliers may stem from and be related to (1) the institutional structure of the economic system, (2) the level of economic development, (3) current monetary policy measures, and (4) relevant current economic developments. This leads to the conclusion that these differences in monetary multipliers are strongly related to the time variable that depends on the period under consideration because the shorter the period, the more the variability of the monetary multipliers. Great differences in relevant ratios at the beginning and end of the period under study may reflect the transfers from the previous period over to the next period. For instance, a large inherited extra supply of reserve money at the beginning of the period under study makes it possible to increase the money supply in spite of a decrease in reserve money. There may be the contrary case of a decrease in the reserve money and an accompanying decrease in the money supply, with a strong increase in reserve money near the end of the period; this appears as a decrease in money supply in spite of the increase in reserve money. As a result, the role of the time dimension is very important, and the solution may be to investigate the monetary multiplication in longer time periods and to try to eliminate the repercussions from inherited or transferred extra reserve money or deficits in reserve money.

Role of Institutional Sectors and Control of the MSP

The concept of the MSP as a complex process in the monetary structure and within other financial transactions in the portfolio selection framework requires an appropriate initial understanding of the motives and behavior of different groups of economic units (institutional sectors). In addition, the motivation and behavior of individual institutional sectors are changing, especially in the economic development process—significant in a comparative analysis of the MSP of an economy. It must be assumed that there are significant differences in the motives and behavior of the individual institutional sectors in the MSP within the different economic systems; this is important not only for a comparative analysis of the MSP but also for an analysis of the individual economies and related institutional changes.

For these reasons, an analysis of the MSP, both national and comparative, has to involve sector consideration of the MSP for a better understanding of it and what causes the relationships in this process along with the control factor.

An appropriate classification of the economic units in the MSP should be used to distinguish the two basic groups involved: financial and nonfinancial units. A further differentiation of financial units should distinguish the monetary institutions and other financial institutions. The monetary institutions are classified into two groups: the central banking system (monetary authorities, including central banking operations of the central government) and the other monetary institutions. Finally, nonfinancial units and other monetary institutions have to be classified into five domestic sectors: central government, other governments, enterprises, households, and the rest of the world.

1. The central banking sector (monetary authorities) decides reserve money creation ($_cA$) partly by transactions in domestic currency ($_cA_d$), and partly by foreign exchange transactions ($_cE_n$). It also influences monetary multiplication by obligatory reserve rates and obligatory deposits of nonmonetary units with the central banking system ($_cT$). Claims on domestic residents on the assets side of the central banking system's balance sheet indicate that the instruments for reserve money creation and items on the liabilities side of this balance sheet explain the holdings structure of reserve money as it experiences the influence of

the central banking system (R_o, $_cT$) and partially reflects the autonomous decisionmaking by other monetary units (R_o) and by the nonmonetary units (C, $_cDM$). Claims and liabilities related to foreign residents explain the influence of foreign exchange transactions on reserve money. A significant indirect influence on the MSP is the central banking system, which can not only perform through its interest rate policy but also influence the portfolio selection behavior of the participants in the MSP.

2. The other monetary institutions determine their domestic investments ($_mA$); the reserve money held on account with the central banking system (R), excluding obligatory reserves; money borrowed from the central banking system ($_cA$) up to the level accepted by this system; and foreign assets and liabilities within the framework of their creditworthiness on the foreign market. The domestic liabilities mainly reflect autonomous decisionmaking by nonmonetary units.

3. The nonmonetary domestic sectors decide how much to borrow within the limits offered by monetary institutions (A) and how much of their assets to hold in currency (C), deposit money (DM), and nonmonetary deposits with monetary institutions or in some other instruments issued by these institutions (T) .

4. A significant characteristic of nonmonetary domestic institutional sectors may be their behavior in demand for money. Initially, it should be assumed that individual institutional sectors have different motives and other demand determinants for money, leading to a different relative demand for money in comparison with other institutional sectors. These may result in different reasons for the assessment of money demand. In addition, these sectors may differ in the degree to which they become aware of and react to deviations in their money holdings of money from their demand for money, considering both the preciseness of adjusting money held to demand for money and the time lag in this adjustment. This may be particularly significant for extra money held. Thus, lower institutional sector sensitivity to demand for money should be assumed through lower leakage of money into nonmonetary deposits of monetary institutions that contribute to a greater ratio k and greater monetary multiplier, greater leakage of reserve money where money is held with the central banking system that contributes to a greater ratio p and lower monetary multiplier, and greater variability of monetary multipliers. (These differences in money held in institutional sectors may be meaningful for a comparative analysis of the different behavior of the institutional sectors in different types of economies.)

5. The foreign sector has an indirect influence on the MSP through the amount of the current account of the balance of payments. This

indirect influence may have a different effect on the MSP as a result of the different involvement of the monetary and nonmonetary units in financing the balance-of-payments transactions.

In the control of the MSP, the basic point to remember is that the MSP is influenced not only by monetary authorities but also by other monetary institutions and nonmonetary units, domestic and foreign. The first question is how this conclusion is related to the strongly prevailing views on the active influence of money quantity on economic developments (money matters) if nonmonetary units, which influence economic developments, are able to affect changes in the money supply; how is it possible that the quantity of money influences their behavior? Instead of the influence of money quantity on their behavior in the demand for goods and services, prices, level of production and employment, exports, and imports, it appears more probable that they determine the adjustment of money quantity to demand for money by influencing its increase or decrease. In other words, if changes in the money supply are influenced by a combination of controlled and autonomous variables, how much indeed can the amount of the money supply and "money matters" be controlled?

The answer to this question is that three levels of control and autonomous influence on money supply have to be distinguished:

1. The central banking system is able to control the maximum level of money supply, mainly by controlling investments of monetary institutions (A), particularly in deciding reserve money creation (c) by reserve rate requirements.

2. Of lesser influence on the quantity of money is decisionmaking by other monetary institutions about the maximum amount of reserve money creation to use and how much they should invest within that framework. In this way, other monetary institutions cannot exceed the maximum level of investments controlled by the central banking system; however, they can go below this level.

3. This involves decisionmaking by nonmonetary units to borrow less than the amount offered by monetary institutions, thereby influencing the quantity of money that would be parallel with their decisionmaking to hold money and invest it in nonmonetary financial instruments.

In this way, monetary authorities are able to control the maximum level of the quantity of money, but autonomous decisionmaking by other monetary institutions, including nonmonetary units, can influence the lower level of the quantity of money. Thus, control over the quantity of money depends on the gap between the maximum level decided by monetary authorities and the minimum level corresponding to demand for money. The narrower the gap, the greater the degree of control over the money supply by monetary authorities. If these authorities are able to make a correct assessment of the demand for money and to create the quantity of reserve money corresponding to this quantity of money, they will have full control over the money supply. On the contrary, if these authorities allow a maximum level significantly beyond the demand for money, their degree of control over the money supply may indeed be minimal.

A complementary rather than exclusive approach appears to allow for the significant role of monetary authorities in the MSP, which parallels that of other monetary institutions and nonmonetary units in the process. This approach eliminates the apparent contradiction between autonomous influences on money supply and its impact on autonomous decisionmaking in real transactions, especially on the maximum level of money supply determined by monetary authorities rather than the demand for money.

Moving closer to the main purpose of the question of control of the MSP, the first conclusion, based on the basic formula of money creation (equation 1) is that the creation of reserve money ($_cA$) may be under the full control of monetary authorities (the central banking system and the central government), if the appropriate monetary regulations of the level of reserve money are applied. Second, the monetary multiplier cannot be controlled as well. The numerator of this multiplier ratio on the right sides of equations 8 and 9 is influenced by the autonomous behavior of other monetary institutions (A, E_n), and that of the nonmonetary units (T, E_n), within the maximum level determined by the monetary authorities. The denominator of this multiplier ratio is also predominately determined by autonomous influences. A significant influence by monetary authorities is possible in holding reserve money by other monetary institutions with the central banking system (entropy of reserve money, R, e) and on obligatory nonmonetary deposits of nonmonetary units with the central banking system ($_ct$). However, the largest and most significant component in holding reserve money or currency in circulation (C) depends on the autonomous decisionmaking of nonmonetary units. In addition, holding deposit money with the central banking system ($_cDM$) in economies where this is the rule depends on autonomous decisionmaking.

For a proper understanding of the function of institutional sectors in the MSP, we need to explain the contradictory nature of their behavior and transactions related to the MSP. The role of macromotivation and behavior of the central banking system (monetary authorities) and the micromotivation and behavior of other institutional sectors involved in the MSP should be recognized. The actions of the central banks are related to the implementation of macrotargets in the money supply (monetary policy targets) involved in the MSP. On the other hand, relevant activities and transactions by other institutional sectors are micromotivated to the neglect of monetary policy macrotargets and monetary authorities.

In view of the complexity of institutional sectors in the MSP, a methodological approach to their analysis deserves attention. From a theoretical and practical view, it appears that interaction of institutional sectors with the classification of transactions makes the flow-of-funds accounts more appealing. Involvement in the financial and nonfinancial transactions also lends support for this conclusion, which is valid for changing economies and comparative analysis. In both cases, the flow-of-funds accounts can be used to show how these changes have affected the institutional sectors and transaction structure of economic changes and the different types of economies in a comparative analysis. The flow-of-funds accounts, serving as a basis for analysis, contribute in a macro and micro sense to the credibility of the analysis. For example, the role of the individual institutional sectors in the MSP in a macro sense (horizontal interrelationships) is more easily explained. However, in a micro sense, the portfolio selection behavior of individual institutional sectors (vertical interrelationships) involving both financial and nonfinancial relationships is better understood. Thus, the combination of macro and micro analysis of the MSP, which is based on a flow-of-funds matrix, offers the optimal conditions for answering questions arising from an analysis of the MSP.

The Influence of Balance-of-Payments Transactions on the MSP

Foreign exchange transactions by monetary institutions represent one of the basic components of the MSP and changes in the money supply that influence reserve money creation ($_cE_n$) and the monetary multiplier (E_n). It is logical to assume that these influences on foreign exchange transactions are closely related to the surplus or deficit of the current account of the balance-of-payments transactions. According to this assumption, a positive balance in the current account should be accompanied by a positive E_n and $_cE_n$ or by the creation of money (E_n) and of reserve money ($_cE_n$) or by the opposite effect in a negative balance in this account.

However, the balance-of-payments current account of the MSP is more complex and far reaching because (1) foreign financial transactions accompanying a surplus or a deficit in this account are performed by three groups of institutions with different roles in the MSP: the central banking system, monetary institutions, and nonmonetary units; and (2) these foreign financial transactions performed in foreign currency between domestic and foreign residents register no monetary effects on the assets and liabilities side of the ledgers. Monetary effects are observed in the buying/selling of foreign exchange by domestic currency between nonmonetary and monetary subjects, the central banking system, and other monetary institutions.

Then, this same account balance may produce a very different monetary effect: a surplus may lead to positive $_cE_n$ and E_n, positive $_cE_n$ and negative E_n, positive E_n and negative $_cE_n$, and negative $_cE_n$ and E_n. The combination that emerges will depend on the involvement of the monetary and nonmonetary subjects in foreign financial transactions. Little effect will be noticed if monetary institutions are not involved in foreign financing. The strongest impact will be registered if monetary institutions are broadly involved in foreign financing transactions and buying and selling of foreign exchange by domestic currency.

Thus, the balance-of-payments transactions influence the MSP indirectly through buying/selling of foreign exchange by domestic currency between the central banking system and other monetary institutions and the monetary institutions and nonmonetary subjects. Changes result in their foreign assets and foreign liabilities, making identification of these effects possible. The balance-of-payments transactions have as much direct influence on the MSP as nonmonetary units less involved in foreign financial transactions. When there aren't any foreign financial transactions by nonmonetary units, the surplus/deficit in the current account of balance of payments shows up on the balance sheets of monetary institutions, reflecting its influence on the MSP. Significant changes in transactions are represented in the share of nonmonetary units in foreign financing, the central banking system, and other monetary institutions in these transactions, which necessarily contribute to significant changes in the reserve money creation structure and in monetary multiplication.

SUMMARY

Designed primarily as the construction model for a comparative analysis of the MSP, this national analysis model for the MSP has been adjusted in the following ways:

1. Selection and differentiation of variables are modified to accommodate a wider variety of these variables encountered in the different types of economies.

2. Analysis of the role of institutional sectors is emphasized to include not only the different behavior of these sectors in individual economies but also the behavior of the individual sectors in different types of economies, particularly in different economic systems.

3. Traditional differentiation of variables and their ratios in the MSP, which is designed for a better understanding and comparison of those involved in reserve money creation and monetary multiplication, is accompanied by a functional differentiation of variables and ratios that involves the concepts of leakage of money and reserve money and entropy of reserve money.

4. The practical application of this empirical analysis has imposed the elimination of variables, ratios, and topics not statistically identified and analyzed in a comparative analysis of one hundred countries with several types of economic systems and levels of economic development.

5. Application of the stock and flow (static and dynamic) approach to an analysis of the MSP appears suitable for comparative analysis. The stock approach relates to portfolio selection behavior as the basic economic background of the MSP, and the flow approach is designed to explain the contributory process to changes in variables and relationships in the stock of the MSP ratios.

Within this framework, the MSP is defined by the equation

$$M \ = \ {}_cA \cdot m \tag{1}$$

as a product of reserve money creation $({}_cA)$ and monetary multiplier (m).

Creation/withdrawal of reserve money $({}_cA)$ is the result of both domestic $({}_cA_d)$ and foreign transactions $({}_cE_n)$ of the central banking system, including relevant transactions by the central government or monetary authorities:

$${}_cA \ = \ {}_cA_g + {}_cA_m + {}_cA_n + {}_cU_a + {}_cE_n \tag{3 and 4}$$

The monetary multiplier (*m*) indicates the result of the elimination process for reserve money imbalance caused primarily by creation/withdrawal of reserve money reflected in the new level (change) in money supply. Mathematically defined as the number of units of money supply per unit of reserve money, the equation of monetary multiplier includes a differentiation of variables and ratios aimed at explaining the influence of types of transactions and institutional sectors on its size and its changes:

$$m \ = \ (1 - t - f) \ : \ (e + c + d + c_t)   \qquad (9)$$

This involves

1. Ratios and variables influenced by
    —the central banking system (*e*)
    —other monetary institutions (*e*)
    —nonmonetary units (domestic and foreign: t, f, c, d, c_t)
2. Variables and ratios representing
    —leakage of money (t, f)
    —leakage of reserve money (c, d, c_t)
    —entropy of reserve money (*e*)

The combined influence of the central banking system (which is responsible for the implementation of monetary policy targets in the development of money supply), other monetary institutions, and nonmonetary units raises the question of money supply control by the central banking system. This may be examined in light of whether (1) the central banking system can determine the maximum level of money supply; (2) other monetary institutions can determine a lower level of money supply than the maximum level determined by the central banking system; and (3) the nonmonetary units are free to decide how much to use this opportunity to borrow and increase the money supply offered by other monetary institutions.

The monetary multiplication process is simplified by the omission of the time variable. Assuming there is a significant variation in reserve money creation, it is possible to have higher or lower, even negative, monetary multipliers, especially in dynamic (flow) multipliers, within relatively short periods of time. Selection of a proper time frame for the investigation can make the results of these variations tolerable.

Finally, an investigation of the role of institutional sectors in the MSP and the need to include other nonmonetary financial transactions and nonfinancial transactions in portfolio selection decisionmaking suggests the use of the flow-of-funds account as a basis for the analysis model for the MSP. This involves both financial and nonfinancial transactions and classifies these transactions by type and institutional sector.

NOTES

1. J. S. Duesenberry, "The Portfolio Approach to the Demand for Money and Other Assets," *The Review of Economics and Statistics, Supplement* (February 1963).

2. This refers to central government involvement in some central banking transactions and issue of currency. The term central banking system is used to mean monetary authorities.

3. Reserve money disequilibrium/imbalance may be created in some other way with the same results. However, the opposite is true when there is a lower amount of reserve money with less demand for it.

4. Thus, if the formula for monetary multiplication includes the time variable, $m = [1 - (1 - e - c - d - ct)^{n}] (e + c + d + ct) : (1 - t + f)$, and it is assumed that $n = \sigma$, the formula has the form of equation 8.

5. Nicholas Georgescu-Roegen, *The Entropy Law and Economic Process* (Cambridge, MA: Harvard University Press, 1971).

2

Comparative Analysis of the Money Supply Process

Based on the MSP concept and analysis model of the MSP in national economies, this chapter is designed to interpret the concept, the need, and targets for a comparative analysis of the MSP, along with key questions we hope this analysis will answer.

THE CONCEPT OF COMPARATIVE ANALYSIS OF THE MONEY SUPPLY PROCESS

A comparative analysis has been designed to explain similarities and differences within the MSP in the various national economies, including a new basic component: different types of economies. This new dimension in the analysis model of the MSP requires very significant adjustments and increases the complexity of the MSP.

Since financial organization is strongly interrelated with the institutional economic system and the level of economic development, the MSP is closely related to the institutional economic system, the level of economic development, and the other part of the financial process and organization. Differences in the MSP of the various economies result from differences in the institutional economic systems and the level of economic development. In addition, one must consider some other differences in the MSP that modify the influence of the institutional economic system and the economic development level, such as random domestic and foreign influences. In this way, comparative analysis of the MSP is primarily designed to explain the differences in the MSP as a

reflection of the differences in the institutional economic system and the
level of economic development, and deviations from conclusions based
on these two general sources of differences in the MSP.

Within this framework, a comparative analysis of the MSP begins with
the same basic analysis equation of the MSP, as shown in chapter 1 by
equation 1, presenting the MSP resulting from the reserve money
creation ($_cA$) and the monetary multiplier (m):

$$M \;=\; _cA \cdot m$$

The second step in a comparative analysis of the MSP includes an
explanation of $_cA$ and m by variables presented in equations in chapters
3, 4, 5, and 8. Three items may appear significant here in a comparative
analysis of the MSP:

— It should be assumed that in some types of economies some
   variables do not exist. The logical solution then may be that the
   parameters accompanying these variables equal zero.

— The content of some variables (definition of money supply and
   reserve money) may be rather different in different types of
   economies. Therefore, uniform definitions of variables must be
   applied regardless of the definitions used in the individual
   economies.

— The main differences logically appear in ratios explaining
   differences in the monetary multipliers presented in equations
   9, 10, and 11 in chapter 1, and in the percent shares of the flows
   of reserve money creation shown in equations 3, 4, and 5 in this
   chapter. These ratios and percent shares then present the differences in the MSP in the different types of economies, revealing
   the differences in the monetary multipliers and in the creation
   of reserve money. The explanatory ratios may prove useful to
   reveal the differences in these ratios and their causes.

The stock and flow (static and dynamic) aspects of the MSP have to
be distinguished in a comparative analysis of the MSP. Even though they
have a similar meaning in a national analysis of the MSP, the stock aspect
reflects the economic behavior of the economic units in a portfolio choice
at a given time, while the flow aspect explains how changes in the stock
monetary multipliers and the reserve money structure are incorporated
within a certain time frame.

The structural and holistic aspects of a comparative analysis of the MSP should be distinguished. The structural aspect is related to the previously defined comparative analysis concept involving an analysis of the differences in the MSP in the economies with different economic systems at different levels of economic development. However, this analysis presumes an understanding of the types of economies (groups of economies classified as a "type" of economy by their institutional economic system and level of economic development) and their MSP characteristics. The logical hypothesis is that variables and ratios in the MSP in one type of economy are not significantly different. This hypothesis may be empirically disproved by the resulting exogenous determinants of the MSP and their endogenous determinants related to the institutional economic system and economic development level. These variations in averages of the MSP ratios in the individual economies within a type of economy may have significant influence over the average ratios relevant to a type of economy and on the structural comparative analysis conclusions of the MSP. An intensive analysis of the MSP within each type of economy appears necessary before a structural analysis of the MSP can begin.

The Objectives of Comparative Analysis of the MSP

A comparative analysis of the MSP focuses on a better understanding of it under a different set of conditions, with valid theoretical and practical rules subject to these conditions in the different economic systems with varying levels of economic development. Comparative analysis of the MSP is expected to define its theoretical rules—valid for all economies—and to define the applicable rules relevant to a practical monetary policy in all economies.

This will mean understanding that the practice and theories related to the MSP in developed economies may be highly sophisticated and, as a result, not necessarily valid in all economies, especially if the application is at a lower level of economic development or in different economic systems. For economies at a lower level of economic development, a comparative analysis of the MSP will contribute to a better understanding of the theoretical and practical aspects of those more highly developed economies in an attempt to incorporate this experience, *mutatis mutandis*, into their own economies.

The results of a comparative analysis of the MSP will be of special interest to international financial organizations so that they can adjust their operations to the different types of economies.

That all of these contributory objectives improve the behavior of monetary practice is increasingly significant in the contemporary climate of the growing independence and heightened differentiation between the economies and the expanding role of international financial institutions in the next decade. To meet these objectives, a comparative analysis of the MSP must include an investigation and definition of the conclusions drawn from the influence of these subjects:

— institutional economic system
— level of economic development
— other influence sources and their random variables

Conclusions about the similarities and differences among the different types of economies and within the same type economy or institutional economic system and the same level of economic development may be applied to (1) the structure of reserve money creation (cA); (2) the monetary multiplier (m); (3) ratios determining the monetary multiplier; (4) influence of the institutional sectors on the MSP, central banking system, other monetary institutions, other domestic institutional sectors, and the rest of the world; (5) the role of control and autonomous variables and ratios in the MSP; (6) the degree of predictability and control of the MSP; (7) explanation of the variations in the size of the variables and ratios in the individual economies and types of economies.

The flow and stock aspect of the MSP should define these conclusions, including the interrelationship between conclusions and changes in the MSP in this period.

The Matrix Approach to Comparative Analysis of the MSP

A comparative study of the MSP analyzes the institutional economic system and the level of economic development as the basic determinants of the MSP to include causes of the differences in the MSP in the different economies. This leads to the conclusion that a comparative analysis of the MSP involving horizontal and vertical vectors should be based on a two-dimensional matrix presentation of the relevant components of the MSP with its foundation in institutional economic systems/development levels.

In this approach, the variables and ratios in the MSP are presented horizontally in the institutional economic systems to form horizontal

Table 2.1
Two-Dimensional Matrix Presentation of a Variable and Ratio

(Variable, Ratio)

The level of economic development	The Economic System				
	A	B	C	...	Arithmetic Mean
1					
2					
3					
. . .					
Arithmetic Mean					

A, B, C = institutional sectors
1, 2, 3 = levels of economic development

vectors involving variables and ratios in the different types of institutional economic systems at the same level of economic development. In addition, variables and ratios relating to economic development levels are presented vertically to form vertical vectors involving variables and ratios at different levels of economic development in the same institutional sector. In this way, the cells in this matrix present the variables and ratios influenced by both the institutional economic systems and the levels of economic development as general determinants. Because the cells also reflect the influence of specific and random determinants and can significantly modify the influence of the institutional economic system and the economic development level, they must be considered.

The two-dimensional matrix has to be prepared for each relevant variable and ratio, which are then calculated as the arithmetic means of the variables and ratios of economies involved in a cell of the matrix. Table 2.1 presents relevant components of the MSP in matrix form.

Based on this matrix, a comparative analysis of the MSP involves

— definition of the hypothesis of the influence of the institutional system and the level of economic development on the MSP and presentation of these hypotheses in table 2.1
— test of the hypothesis horizontally and vertically with pertinent empirical evidence in the matrix form
— explanation of the deviations from the hypothesis resulting from exogenous and random causes
— final conclusions on the role played by the institutional sectors, level of economic development, and other subjects in the comparative analysis of the MSP.

Additional details on the application of this approach to a comparative analysis of the MSP may be found in chapters 5 and 6 and particularly in chapter 7.

3

Classification of Economies

The comparative analysis of the MSP in this book is based on the hypothesis of the institutional economic system and the economic development level of an economy as a basic determinant for the MSP. These two general determinants of the MSP will be defined in this chapter as the criteria for a classification of the economies for a comparative and structural analysis of the MSP and the economies involved. For a better understanding of the conclusions of this analysis, an explanation follows the appropriate economies classified by these criteria.

INSTITUTIONAL ECONOMIC SYSTEM AND ECONOMIC DEVELOPMENT LEVEL

This section addresses four topics: (1) existing definitions of the economic system, (2) the definitions of the institutional economic system, (3) economic development level for the requirements of this analysis, and (4) classification of the economies by definition of the institutional economic system and economic development level.

The Economic System: Definitions and Classification

For the purpose of this study, the economic system can be defined as an "evolving complex of organizations of participants concerned with the disposal of scarce resources for the satisfaction of private and collective wants."[1] Thus, the economic system is defined as a complex of interacting participants and their organizations in decisionmaking on production, pricing, income distribution, savings, investments, and other economic operations as motivated by a set of interests, rules, and government measures.[2]

Two parts of an economic system become distinguishable: the "real infrastructure" and the "financial superstructure."[3] While a determinant of the financial superstructure, the real infrastructure involves the basic institutional (economic, political, ideological) components of the economic system while the financial superstructure includes the structure of financial institutions and financial instruments. Since it is closely related to the MSP, the financial superstructure of the economic system is of prime interest in this study. Consequently, the real infrastructure is explained here only to the extent that it determines the financial superstructure of the economic system. Both of them are considered in a "positive," not "normative," sense.

Two parts of the real infrastructure emerge: the institutional infrastructure and the level of economic development.

The institutional infrastructure of the economic system (institutional/economic system) mainly involves

— ownership of the means of production, indicating a capitalist or socialist economic system, ideology, and relevant motivation of economic behavior

— economic decisionmaking structured on the level of production, pricing of goods and services, income distribution, savings, investment, financial transactions, and foreign transactions

— integration mechanisms, including free markets, central planning mechanism, or a combination of both

— the types of economic units classified by institutional sector, reflecting the components of an economic system through private/socialist enterprise, government role in economic regulation, role of the rest of the world, and the household transaction structure

The economic infrastructure of the economic system relates to these levels through

— economic development level, entrepreneurial efficiency, labor and capital productivity, production structure, balance-of-payments transactions, and balances of current accounts; supply/demand elasticities; function of pricing and integration mechanisms

— analysis of the per capita gross national product (GNP) used as a basic criterion for classification of the economy by economic development level

The glaring exception is the classification of developing economies as "oil exporters" while responding to the not insignificant influence of the balance-of-payments transactions of the MSP.

Classification of Economies by Institutional Economic System

The literature of comparative economic systems contains several approaches to the classification of economic systems. The most simple but unacceptable approach is that the economic system defined as normal is the orthodox capitalist economic system based on perfect market competition and an "invisible" hand guiding all economic processes. There are variations on this economic system in practice, but the tendency is to eliminate them while moving closer to a normal system.

An obvious inconsistency in this concept—the existing differentiation of economic systems—has led to a two-tiered approach in the classification of economic systems. The assertion is that all economic systems should be classified somewhere between two opposite poles on a line featuring on one end the capitalist economic system, which is based on the freedom to make economic decisions on private ownership, means of production, and perfect market competition, and on the other the socialist economies with full public ownership of the means of production, full government command of economic developments, and central planning. In reality the economic system of the United States represents the first and that of the USSR the second. All of the other countries have been classified somewhere in between by their market affinity or the government influence on economic developments.

Other classifications based on this approach include (1) economic systems with exclusive private ownership of means of production, and (2) economic systems with exclusive public ownership of the means of production on the other end of the spectrum.

However, the appearance of developing economies and the diversification of both capitalist and socialist economies have led to a more flexible classification of economic systems: (1) free market economic systems, (2) socialist central planning economic systems, and (3) economic systems of developing economies. Four groups of economic systems then follow:

— traditional free market economic systems
— free market economic systems with socialist governments
— economic systems with a significant part of public (nationalized) enterprises in the economy
— economic systems of developing economies and socialist central planning economic systems

The third and perhaps most advanced approach considers all of these classifications to be oversimplified. The differentiated structure of today's economic systems imposes a more differentiated classification of the economic systems that will fully reflect the multidimensional structure of an economic system. Therefore, the classification for the economic systems should be based on a multidimensional structure. However, there is no practical solution to the multidimensional approach to the problem of classifying economic systems.

For the purpose of this analysis of the MSP, the classification of economies is a two-dimensional matrix with vectors based on a classification of the economies in an institutional economic system and vectors based on economic development levels.

The classification of economies by institutional economic system in this MSP study has to consider the complex structure of the institutional components. A simplified but practical solution to this problem is the realistic presumption that the degree of freedom and decentralized economic decisionmaking may be considered representative of the institutional economic system. The other characteristic of the institutional economic system, combined with some economic freedom, is the ownership of the means of production; this reflects the capitalist socialist components of the economic system.

Based on this presumption, the practical but useful classification of economies in institutional economic systems may include three types in decreasing order of freedom and decentralization of economic decisionmaking: (1) capitalist economies, (2) socialist economies with decentralized economic decisionmaking, and (3) socialist economies with centralized economic decisionmaking.

Further subclassification of institutional economic systems would lead to an overlapping of the subsystems that may overly complicate the

Table 3.1
GNP at Market Prices by Income Group

Income Group (US dollars)	Population mid-1980 (millions)	GNP 1980 (billions of US dollars)	Average GNP per capita (1980 US dollars)
Less than 360	2,056	505	245
360 to 829	396	211	533
830 to 3,539	655	1,133	1,730
3,540 to 8,269	141	767	5,435
8,270 and over	630	6,851	10,874

Source: "Gross National Product, Population and Growth," Atlas (Washington, DC: World Bank, 1983).

comparative analysis. As a result, the solution is to base the classification of economies on the above three basic types of economic systems.

Classification by Economic Development

The concept of economic development level has its own structural characteristics. However, we assume in this book that the per capita GNP provides a practical indication of the basic level of economic development. Using the World Bank classification of economies based on per capita GNP in 1980, five groups of economies should be considered (see table 3.1).

Classification by per capita GNP does not include the large oil exporters (OPEC), which would appear at the highest level of economic development. To avoid the disturbing effects of these economies, the classification of economies by per capita GNP only is modified by using the classifications made by the International Monetary Fund (*International Financial Statistics*). The combined classification in this analysis is based on a classification of all economies involved in two basic groups: industrial economies with a per capita GNP of more than $4,600 and developing economies. Then, this group of developing economies is classified into two separate groups, oil exporters and non-oil-exporters, with the non–oil-exporting economies further classified based on per capita GNP.

Another source for deviations of the ratios from the hypothesis may be those variables emanating from the smaller economies; however, problems may be avoided by excluding countries with populations of less than about two million. (Many in this group do not have a monetary system.)

Two-Dimensional Classification of Economies

The combined classification by institutional economic system and level of economic development is presented in the two-dimensional matrix in table 3.2.

According to table 3.2, the economies are classified into 15 groups, if total non–oil-exporting developing economies are not considered. On the other hand, it may be a nine-group classification if all of the non–oil-exporting developing economies are considered as a group, with the subclassified economies per GNP being considered as subgroups of the economies. An empirical investigation may use both of these approaches.

The rows of this matrix (horizontal vectors) present the effects of different types of institutional economic systems. The columns (vertical vectors) indicate the effects of the level of economic development and related economic characteristics. The individual cells represent those economies under the influence of a type of institutional economic system and level of economic development.

Some cells in this matrix are empty because there are no economies of that type. For example, there are no socialist economies with decentralized economic decisionmaking at the economic development level corresponding to "industrial economies." This is the result of an unfortunate dirth of statistical information on these economies, which is especially true of the socialist central planning economies that do not publish the necessary statistical information for an empirical analysis of the MSP. (Three countries of this group who are the exception are members of the International Monetary Fund.) Although the empty cells obviously make conclusions less general, they are still valuable to the study. If the conclusions for horizontal and vertical vectors are reliable enough, these cells can then be estimated by extrapolating these vectors and presenting logically expected parameters for the missing groups of economies.

Table 3.2
Classification of Economies by Institutional Economic System and Level of Economic Development (Number of Countries)

Institutional economic system / Level of economic development	Capitalist economies (CE)	Socialist decentralized economies (SDE)	Socialist centralized economies (SCE)	TOTALS
1. Industrial economies--more than $4,600 per capita GNP	19			19
2. Oil-exporting economies	9			9
3. Developing economies, non-oil-exporting total	61	8	3	72
4. $830-$4,600 US dollars per capita GNP	26	2	2	30
5. $360-$829 US dollars per capita GNP	13	4		22
6. Less than $360 US dollars per capita GNP	22	2	1	25
7. Totals	89	8	3	100

Source: International Financial Statistics.

The matrix classification of economies in table 3.2 also shows the rather asymmetric distribution of economies, especially by institutional economic system. For example, 89 percent are capitalist; 8 percent, socialist with decentralized economic decisionmaking; and 3 percent, socialist with centralized economic decisionmaking. Because the economies involved represent full populations, not sample ones, the relatively small number of economies in some cells does not significantly weaken the conclusions as in a sample population.

CHARACTERISTICS OF ECONOMIES

This section explains the group characteristics of economies classified in individual cells of the matrix in table 3.3. It is designed to (1) facilitate a comparative analysis of the MSP, and (2) contribute to a better understanding of its conclusions. The characteristics of these economies will be explained as they relate to the comparative analysis of the MSP. However, for simplification, the characteristics of an economy at the highest level of economic development is explained in each institutional economic system. An explanation of the characteristics of economies at a lower level of economic development involves just the differences in comparison to those at the highest levels of economic development in the same institutional economic system. According to the MSP concept of comparative analysis, these explanations involve first the institutional/financial infrastructure, including the foreign exchange system, followed by the economic/financial and foreign transactions structure.

Capitalist Economies

The institutional infrastructure of industrial economies of more than $4,600 per capita GNP includes this framework:

— *Private ownership of the means of production.* In many countries there is a significant number of nationalized enterprises, particularly those with special national interests and significant government role in ownership of the means of production—this is found in countries with a socialist party in control of government.

— *Economic decisionmaking.* It is decentralized but increases government economic intervention through indirect and direct economic policy measures.

— *Integration mechanisms.* They provide avenues for the creation of efficient free markets for goods and services in financial channels, foreign exchange, and labor markets.

Table 3.3
Economies Involved in a Comparative Analysis of the MSP

Industrial economies

Australia	Guatemala	Pakistan	Greece
Austria	Israel	Rwanda	Niger
Belgium	Jordan	Sierra Leone	New Zealand
Canada	Jamaica	Somalia	Netherlands
Denmark	Korea	Sri Lanka	Tunisia
Lebanon	Togo	Finland	Turkey
Malaysia	Uganda	France	Peru
Mexico	Zaire	Sweden	Portugal
United Kingdom	South Africa	Switzerland	Singapore
United States	Spain	Norway	Spain
Germany	Japan	Paraguay	Italy
Ireland			

Oil-exporting economies

Algeria	Nigeria
Indonesia	Oman
Kuwait	Saudi Arabia
Libya	United Arab
Venezuela	Emirates

Capitalist Non-oil-exporting developing economies

$830–4,600 per capita GNP	$360–829 per capita GNP	Less than $360 per per capita GNP
Argentina	Bolivia	Bangladesh
Brazil	Cameroon	Benin
Chile	Egypt	Burkina Faso
Colombia	El Salvador	Burma
Congo	Ghana	Burundi
Costa Rica	Honduras	Central African Republic
Cote d'Ivoire	Kenya	Chad
Dominican Republic	Papua New Guinea	Haiti
Ecuador	Philippines	India
	Senegal	Madagascar
	Sudan	Malawi
	Thailand	Mali
	Yemen Arab Republic	Nepal

Socialist economies with decentralized economic decisionmaking

$830–4,600 per capita GNP	$360–829 per capita GNP	Less than $360 per capita GNP
Syrian Arab Republic	Nicaragua	Ethiopia
Yugoslavia	Yemen P. D. Republic	Tanzania
	Zambia	
	Zimbabwe	

Socialist economies with centralized economic decisionmaking

$830–4,600 per capita GNP	Less than $360 per capita GNP
Hungary	China

Source: International Financial Statistics.

The financial superstructure is characterized by a decentralized structuring of the different types of financial institutions involving a (1) central banking system, (2) other monetary institutions (commercial banks), (3) savings institutions, (4) investment banks, (5) industrial banks, (6) insurance institutions, (7) investment trusts, (8) open market institutions, and (9) agents in share and bond markets. This framework is found mainly in private ownership but also in public ownership designed for specific government intervention on a domestic and foreign scale that includes:

— *Differentiated financial instrument structure*. This is focused particularly on securities that are negotiable on the financial market.
— *Foreign exchange transactions*. There is freedom here running parallel with freedom in balance-of-payments transactions (financial and current) and convertible domestic currency.

The economic characteristics pertinent to an MSP analysis include:

— *Asymmetric sector distribution*. This appears in savings and investments as they are reflected in a higher rate of financial savings per household, with negative financial savings by enterprises. That this financial intermediation is the essential precondition for an efficient working economy becomes apparent.
— *Monetary disequilibrium/imbalance*. There may be significant disturbances in economic development affecting demand for goods and services, price of goods and services, production, exports, and imports. Consequently, the efficient control of monetary aggregates represents one of the basic components of economic policy.
— *Financial transactions*. They lead to, first, a relatively high level of financial flows, assets, and liabilities reflected in the high financial flows and financial assets ratio to GNP.[4] Second, highly institutionalized financial flows are mirrored in the large share claimed by financial institutions in total financial flows and assets, with a smaller portion claimed by monetary institutions in these flows, assets, and liabilities. This is a result of the largely developed structure and operations of nonmonetary financial institutions and nonmonetary financial instruments further reflected in the small portion of (a) monetary instruments in total financial instruments, (b) the smaller amount of currency in circulation in total money supply, and (c) less participation by

the central banking system in financial transactions, assets, and liabilities because of concentrated operations with other monetary institutions and the central government cause less borrowing by other monetary institutions. The third effect is the differentiated structure of financial market transactions.

— *Market function.* These are highly integrated markets, with consistent valuation in the four basic markets through (1) development of prices on markets for goods and services, (2) interest rates on the financial market, (3) foreign exchange rates on their market, and (4) wages on the labor market. The efficient operation and function of integrated markets makes the differentiated and autonomous portfolio selection process possible, including the demand for money and nonmonetary financial assets.

— *Stability of parameters.* The ratios revealed here reflect the relevant relationships between transactions, assets, and reasonably stable liabilities.

Developing Economies

The developing economies are found in countries with a per capita GNP of less than $4,600 U.S. dollars and include these characteristics:

— *Institutional.* This institutional infrastructure in comparison with industrial economies experiences (1) increased government economic intervention through direct economic policy measures; (2) less efficient integration mechanisms revealed by a disintegrated financial market and foreign exchange market, with no uniform pricing; (3) low differentiation in financial institutions and instruments in securities through the central bank and other monetary institutions, with no open market institutions; and (4) extensive regulation of foreign exchange transactions and balance-of-payments transactions emphasizing imports and foreign borrowing.

— *Economic.* A comparative analysis of the MSP will reveal that (1) their rate of financial flows and assets (lower financial assets by GNP rate or FIR) is lower than that of the industrial economies; (2) monetary institutions represent the main financial institutions in performing most financial transactions; (3)

central banking operations within monetary institutions play a major role in the financial transactions of monetary institutions with nonfinancial domestic and foreign subjects; (4) other monetary institutions borrow heavily from the central bank and are greatly dependent on it for their credit capacity, which is very important in the MSP; (5) a low profile of financial and foreign exchange market operations results from domestic currency that is nonconvertible or almost nonconvertible within the normal conversion range; and (6) there is an overall deficit in balance-of-payments current account and capital imports.

In comparison with industrial economies, these differences are even greater at lower levels of economic development. They are not as prominent in economic groups with a per capita GNP closer to $4,600 U.S. dollars but are certainly more pronounced in those economic groups on the lower end of the economic development scale at less than $360 U.S. dollars per capita GNP.

Oil-Exporting Economies

The oil-exporting economies are similar to both industrial and developing economies. There is a similarity to industrial economies in per capita GNP (some have a higher per capita GNP than any industrial economy) and current balance-of-payments account transactions. They also have characteristics in common with a majority of the developing economies. On one hand, these economies cannot be classified as industrial economies since their institutional and economic structure does not function as well. Neither can they be classified as developing economies since most have a very high per capita GNP. Therefore, the classification of these economies into a separate group appears to be the best pragmatic solution—one that eliminates them from the economic groups classified by per capita GNP. This eliminates some deviations in the multipliers and ratios in the MSP, if the role of balance-of-payments transactions becomes one of the significant components of the MSP, although there is a low homogeneity in other characteristics.

Socialist Economies with Decentralized Economic Decisionmaking

The socialist economies with decentralized economic decisionmaking and the highest level of per capita GNP ($830-$4,600 U.S. dollars) will be considered first. Institutional characteristics, which are a part of the institutional infrastructure, include:

— *Ownership*. The means of production is predominantly under public or government or some other type of social ownership in the areas of industry, mining, and transportation, although there is a significant amount of private ownership in agriculture and small firms, e.g., handicraft, services, and transportation.

— *Economic decisionmaking*. This is a decentralized operation, although the government's role in the decisionmaking process of socialist enterprises is indeed significant. There is extensive use of direct and indirect economic policy measures within the framework of indicative economic planning.

— *Integration mechanisms*. These operate normally through an essential market role parallel with economic planning and government intervention. However, at this economic development level, there is a relatively moderate market activity for goods and services, with financial and foreign exchange markets occupying a low-key role.

The financial superstructure within the decentralized economic decisionmaking process is characterized by:

— *Structure of financial institutions*. They are decentralized but not very differentiated. Along with the central banking system, this structure includes commercial banks and specialized banks, since all financial institutions are in public ownership. Semifinancial intermediaries play a significant role in receiving resources from taxes and similar obligatory sources, granting credits per government plans, collecting resources by financial instruments, and allocating resources to public users in the form of "grants." Public ownership of financial institutions and their nonprofit operation motives expose financial institutions to power liquidity and bankruptcy risks, leading to overexpansion of credit in financial institutions (low demand for reserve money holdings with the central banking system). A financial market that does not function well causes monetary institutions to become overly dependent on funds borrowed from the central banking system, which serves only to strengthen the monetary control of the central banking system.

— *Financial instrument structure*. This is nominally differentiated; however, in practice, it mainly involves bilateral instruments almost exclusive of securities as a significant financial instrument, including a simplified monetary aggregate structure.

— *Foreign exchange transactions (nonconvertible domestic currency)*. These are extensively regulated and very narrow transactions of foreign exchange causing monetary institutions to become the main holders of foreign exchange. This has a direct effect on current balance-of-payments transactions, which are extensively regulated on the import side, in the MSP.

The relevant economic characteristics for an analysis of the MSP include:

— *High rate of asymmetry in sector distribution*. This results from a concentration of investments in socialist enterprises running parallel with a high rate of savings by households within the framework of decentralized decisionmaking on income distribution. This imbalance is reflected as high negative financial savings by socialist enterprises with relatively high positive financial savings by households. This process requires efficient financial intermediation.

— *Monetary disequilibrium (imbalance)*. This factor may significantly influence price development, production, imports, and exports—mainly through its influence on domestic demand for goods and services, resulting in the need for efficient planning and implementation of monetary policy goals and targets.

— *High level of financial transactions*. This is revealed through intermediation in assets and liabilities, and the appropriate high ratio of these operations to the GNP. An accompanying factor is the high degree of institutionalization in financial transactions, assets, and liabilities, a result of the strict parameters imposed on nonfinancial units to perform direct financial operations mainly in trade and consumer credits—the major share is taken by monetary institutions, resulting from low differentiation in financial institutions. With this background, that includes an inefficient financial market, other monetary institutions have depended strongly on the central banking system, as reflected in the relatively high rate of borrowing by these institutions. Greater involvement by the central banking system in the operations of nonmonetary institutions generates more influence and control for it in the financial transactions, assets, and liabilities of these monetary institutions. These financial transactions are in a simplified structure that includes bilateral instruments and a large share of money in total financial assets, with a small amount of currency in circulation in the total money supply because the use of deposit money by socialist enterprises predominates in payments (obligatory use of deposit money for interpayments in some economies).

— *Balance-of-payments transactions*. These reflect the deficit in the current account of balance-of-payments and the appropriate imports of capital. The result has been greater foreign liabilities than assets in the monetary institutions, the only holders of foreign exchange reserves. Strong fluctuation in the current account deficit as revealed in the variations of the monetary impact, usually in the form of money supply and reserve money withdrawals, has heightened uncertainties about the creation of money.

— *Market workings*. This process shows the low degree of integration in the goods and services markets, which is reflected in distorted relative prices resulting partly from government price control. In addition, financial and foreign exchange markets have not played a significant role. The portfolio selection process is rather simplified, distorted by the inconsistent valuation of financial instruments and foreign exchange assets, interest rates, and foreign exchange rates.

— *Stability of parameters*. This has been low, resulting in part from economic growth, frequent direct government economic intervention, and changes in economic legislation.

Socialist Economies with Decentralized Economic Decisionmaking (Lower Level of Economic Development)

The lower level of economic development is occupied by economies with less than $830 U.S. dollars per capita GNP. They present the following characteristics:

— *Institutional*. This infrastructure is characterized by (1) the greater role played by government in intervention through direct economic policy measures; (2) influence on the function of socialist enterprises; (3) a more disintegrated market for goods and services; (4) less differentiated financial institutional structure; (5) greater role of the central banking system in financial intermediation and specialized banks and semifinancial intermediaries; and (6) a stronger regulation of balance-of-payments and foreign exchange transactions.

— *Economic characteristics*. They are relevant for an MSP analysis similar to that of economies above the $829 U.S. dollar per capita GNP level, though significant differences exist in (1) a lower ratio of savings by households that require greater involvement in foreign capital imports;(2) a stronger role for monetary disequilibrium in domestic demand for goods and services and prices; (3) lower financial assets—GNP ratio; (4) greater role for monetary institutions in financial intermediation and the central banking system within these institutions; (5) more simplified financial assets structure and financial transactions, with a greater share of money in financial assets and currency in circulation in the money supply; (6) greater deficit in the balance-of-payments current account and more direct monetary influence on balance-of-payments transactions; and (7) inefficient market operation for goods and services.

Socialist nations with decentralized economic decisionmaking reflect their specific economic system and lower level of economic development more than industrial economies. It is logical to compare these economies with capitalist economies at a similar level of economic development, not with industrial economies. In addition, this group of economies has a significantly more differentiated institutional economic system than capitalist economies. This is a result of the different approaches to the concept of a rapidly evolving socialist economy with significant modifications in the institutional economic structure because of their practical experience. Therefore, it is logical to expect greater differences in relevant ratios in the MSP in these economies than in the capitalist economies.

Socialist Economies with Centralized Economic Decisionmaking

The socialist economic system with centralized economic decisionmaking, a "central planning system," is primarily an orthodox system. Recent reforms of this system and their implementation need to be explained. Since the level of economic development will not cause significant modifications to this system, there will be no need to explain economies at different economic development levels.

Orthodox Systems

Orthodox systems have the following institutional characteristics:

— *Public ownership*. This includes the means of production and land.

— *Economic decisionmaking*. This process is effected through centralized decisionmaking within the framework of mandatory central planning, which is focused on certain targeted areas in production, prices of goods and services, income distribution, savings, investments, foreign transactions, and financial transactions. Free private markets for goods and services have limited input, if any, in this process.

— *Integration mechanism*. This operates through central mandatory economic planning, and free private markets for goods and services have a small role.

The financial superstructure involves the centralized banking system, which includes specialized banks. This system performs all bank operations, including crediting of socialist enterprises and other nonfinancial subjects, through the central credit plan. These banks perform credit operations in exports and foreign exchange transactions. The central banking system represents the whole monetary system (there are no other monetary institutions).

— *Financial instruments*. This rather simplified structure includes bank credits, deposit money, other deposits, and currency in circulation. Money instruments have a dual character. First, deposit money is held and used by socialist enterprises and other socialist institutions for payments for planned transactions; extra quantities of money have no effect on demand for goods and services, prices, and other economic developments. Second, it includes currency in circulation, which is held by individuals in order to perform money functions; the extra quantity of money affects the demand for goods and services. In this respect, deposit money represents "accounting" money while currency

in circulation, mainly in the hands of households, represents the
regular fiat money—similar to money in economic systems that
have decentralized economic decisionmaking.
— *Foreign exchange system*. This involves a fully centralized
  system of foreign exchange transactions, including nonconvertible currency.

The economic characteristics related to the MSP include:

— *Asymmetric sector distribution*. In savings and investments in
  these economies, it is specific. The whole (planned) savings in
  socialist enterprises are transferred to central funds. Then, they
  are allocated to socialist enterprises/investors through grants
  and minimal short-term credit. Basically, a low percentage of
  households and private firms engage in savings and investments,
  which does not leave much room for financial intermediation.
— *Monetary disequilibrium*. This force plays a dual role in deposit
  money in socialist entity accounts where there is less money
  than demand for it. Less money, in turn, may generate repayment
  difficulties. When there is more or extra money, it cannot
  generate a greater demand for goods and services because of
  central planning. However, monetary disequilibrium in currency
  in circulation may impact significantly on the demand for goods
  and services. An extra quantity of money beyond the demand
  for money may be expected to lead to an increase in the demand
  for goods and services, although the increased demand cannot
  influence prices, production, or exports and imports, which are
  again centrally planned. Its effect can be observed in the
  reduction or scarcity of goods, causing shortages and the
  disappearance of some products from the market. An additional
  development may be observed in central planning, whereby
  either production must adjust to the demand for goods or the
  quantity of currency in circulation must be corrected. A specific
  "cash plan" mechanism designed to regulate the quantity of
  currency in circulation in these economies takes care of the
  adjustments.
— *Financial transactions*. These operations mirror the character
  of the institutional infrastracture and financial superstructure in
  a logical and precise manner. Low financial assets, liabilities,
  and transactions result from a negligible share of financial

intermediation in the transfer of savings by savers to investors—mainly grants by central funds. All financial transactions are performed by the central banking system and specialized banks, nearly excluding interbank crediting that affects monetary multiplication, which is different from monetary multiplication in a decentralized monetary system. The simplified structure of financial transactions mainly involve bank credits and deposits, with the major part of the money in financial assets and a small amount of currency in circulation in the total money supply because social entities are obliged to use deposit money for payments and are allowed to hold only specified small amounts of currency.

— *Market function.* There is no significant role for the markets, although there is some room for leadership in private production (private markets). Central planning controls the markets for goods and services, financial markets, foreign exchange markets, and labor markets. As a result, relative prices for goods and services are significantly distorted, causing the need for subsidies when prices are low. Interest rates, foreign exchange rates, and wages are centrally planned regardless of the economic interrelationships existing in market economies.

It appears that the MSP of socialist economies with central economic decisionmaking is a simple one addressing mainly the creation of reserve money by the central banking system, with negligible monetary multiplication. This is primarily the result of an almost monobanking system, with central banks performing the role of both monetary authorities and commercial banks. The simplified structure of financial instruments and relatively low volume of financial flows have contributed to a simplification of the MSP in these economies. However, there is an observable differentiation in the MSP because of the duality of money involving regular fiat money in households and private firms and accounting money in socialist enterprises and other socialist (public) entities that make the MSP rather specific.

Reforms (Up to 1983)

There have been reforms in socialist economies with centralized economic decisionmaking involving changes in the institutional infrastructure:

— *Ownership of the means of production*. This entails a more liberal attitude toward private ownership of small firms and farms.

— *Economic decisionmaking*. This calls for greater involvement by socialist enterprises in decisions about production, prices, income distribution, savings, investments, and financial transactions, with a greater role in economic decisionmaking by private producers.

— *Integration mechanisms*. There needs to be more market participation in goods and services (socialist and private); there is no role for financial and foreign exchange markets.

— *Financial superstructure*. There have been no significant changes in the structure of financial institutions and financial instruments, with no meaningful changes in the foreign exchange system and transactions.

Relevant economic characteristics for the MSP include:

— *Asymmetric sector distribution*. There was an increase in asymmetry of sector distribution of savings and investments because of (1) greater freedom in economic decisionmaking by socialist enterprises; (2) larger incomes and savings by households, private firms, and farms; (3) an expanded role for financial intermediation as an instrument for the transfer of savings to investors; and (4) a diminished role for central investment funds and grants.

— *Financial transactions*. They are a mirror for the slight changes that occur in the structure of financial institutions as they reflect the corresponding changes in the financial transactions structure, although the growing need for financial intermediation leads to increased financial assets/transactions ratio to GNP. The presence of the centralized banking system is apparent in centrally controlled financial transactions and the elimination of interbank financial transactions.

— *Market operations*. A broader market role has been displayed in goods and services, although the government's dominant role in price regulation is still evident; there are no financial and foreign exchange markets. The interest rates and foreign exchange rates are centrally decided.

— *Stability of parameters*. Significant institutional changes have
brought about a greater variability in the relevant parameters.

For an analysis of the MSP, it is important that changes in the socialist
economic systems within these reforms be negligibly related to the
financial/monetary systems, which remain almost fully centralized, with
nearly the same MSP characteristics found in orthodox central planning
systems. Therefore, MSP in reforms does not require a separate interpretation of the MSP from that presented in the case of orthodox socialist
economic systems with centralized economic decisionmaking.

NOTES

1. A. G. Gruchy, *Comparative Economic System*, 2d ed. (Boston: Houghton
Mifflin, 1977): 9–11.
2. N. Georgescu-Roegen, *Analytical Economics* (Cambridge, MA: Harvard University Press, 1966).
3. Terminology applied by R. Goldsmith, *Financial Structure and Development*
(New Haven, CT: Yale University Press, 1969).
4. Instead of ratio to GNP, it is possible to apply the "financial interrelations ratio"
(FIR), introduced by R. Goldsmith (see note 3) presenting financial assets to total
assets ratio. However, the FIR, while not under observation, is of little practical use
in most of the economies involved in this study.

4

Compilation of Comparative
Flow-of-Funds Accounts

Flow-of-funds accounts are used in this study as (1) the basis for a methodological concept of the comparative study of the MSP; and (2) a resource for statistical information for an empirical investigation within this methodological framework. Therefore, the compilation of comparative flow-of-funds accounts for economies involved in this study is the first step in a comparative analysis of the MSP based on statistical information presented in the *International Financial Statistics* (IFS) of the International Monetary Fund. It is the only practically applicable statistical publication presenting comparative information on relevant transactions of the economies under study.[1] It determines the basic structure of the flow-of-funds accounts selected for the institutional sectors and types of transactions. These flow-of-funds accounts are prepared for publication by the National Bank of Yugoslavia.

INSTITUTIONAL SECTORS

Statistical information in the IFS is suitable to appropriately classify monetary institutions, although it is far less differentiated when applied to the existing flow-of-funds accounts in individual economies.

The monetary institutions sector includes two subsectors: central banking system and other monetary institutions.

— *Central banking system.* This includes any monetary operations by the central government, such as the "issuance of currency or the holding of international reserves and positions vis-à-vis the Fund,"2 that involve this sector in the whole monetary structure.

— *Other monetary institutions.* This subsector includes commercial and other banks that have large demand deposits. These are banks that participate significantly in the monetary and credit multiplication process as institutions creating money by their credits on the assets side of their balance sheet and generating money on the liabilities side of their balance sheet (deposit money).

Based on statistical information provided for the IFS on the classification of economic units by institutional sector, statistical information provided by IFS appears to be basically consistent with a comparative analysis of the MSP role in the monetary institutions process.

Classification of financial and nonfinancial and nonmonetary units must be simplified: (1) it is not possible to construct a sector involving nonmonetary financial institutions because there is insufficient comparative statistical data on transactions by these institutions; and (2) it is not possible to separate enterprises, corporations, or quasi-corporations or individual firms from households.

Since both of these groups of economic units are presented in the "private sector" by IFS, domestic nonmonetary units can be classified in only the two sectors: central government and other domestic sectors.

The central government sector includes all government transactions, with the exception of monetary transactions. Other domestic sectors include nonfinancial and financial nonmonetary sector transactions, including nonclassified transactions, errors, and omissions in the residual sector.

Statistical information on balance-of-payments transactions in the IFS provides a compilation of the rest of the world sector. This involves comparisons of foreign residents and classification of transactions for MSP analysis.

The classification of economic units by institutional sector is simplified; however, it is suitable for an uncomplicated financial analysis of the MSP that consists of the appropriate classification of monetary institutions and nonmonetary units that satisfies the needs of the above model.

The MSP analysis involves two basic groups of nonmonetary units: nonmonetary domestic units and foreign residents. The central government and other domestic units fall within the domestic nonmonetary units.

TYPES OF TRANSACTIONS

Classifications and definitions of the transactions used in this MSP analysis have to be adjusted to the model and available information sources. These adjustments to the analysis model require some modifications of transactions (assets and liabilities) definitions. For instance, the definition of reserve money created by the central banking system ($_cA$) is different from the definition of reserve money held by other monetary institutions (R) and reserve money meaning leakage of it from the MSP (currency in circulation, deposit money with the central banking system, and other liabilities of the central banking system) as variables involved in the monetary multiplier. As sources of information, the definitions and classification of transactions have to be adjusted to those used in the *International Financial Statistics* (International Monetary Fund), which represent the only comparative source of information on transactions involved in the MSP. The result is a more simplified classification of these transactions, even more than the national analysis of the MSP, but also differentiated enough to provide for the basic types of transactions in the MSP, making possible an analysis of the MSP based on the above mode. The main simplification is the omission of (1) a more detailed differentiation of nonmonetary liabilities of monetary institutions, and (2) omissions of financial transactions outside monetary institutions (intercrediting, issue and holding of securities by nonmonetary units). However, the omission of these transactions does not create an essential limitation of an analysis of the MSP.

Using this approach, the following classification of transactions is used in the MSP:

— *Reserve money*. The country pages of the *International Financial Statistics* include deposits of other monetary institutions with the central banking system that include obligatory reserves and cash in vaults of these institutions and their holding of foreign currency used in the domestic economy as legal tender. Securities qualifying as assets under secondary reserve requirements are not included. Defined in this way, reserve money is included as a monetary multiplier variable R.

— *Creation of reserve money or total reserve money*. This includes total assets of the central banking system, net of foreign liabilities, and net of other liabilities, if they are less than other assets. Defined in this way, total reserve money is included in the formula of creation of money as the variable $_cA$.

— *Money supply*. Deposit money and currency in circulation compose this category. Deposit money is defined in a narrow sense to include only transferable deposits used as instruments of payment and held by domestic units with monetary institutions (central banks and other monetary institutions). However, the exception is deposits held by the central government. Currency in circulation encompasses notes and coins outside banks.

— *Quasi-money*. This includes deposits with monetary institutions not used as a means of payment or time and sight savings deposits and foreign exchange deposits by domestic residents that are convertible into money with little delay and without financial penalty upon presentation to the issuer.

— *Other liabilities*. This mainly covers the liabilities of monetary institutions in (1) bonds and money market instruments issued by monetary institutions, (2) import and restricted deposits, (3) central government deposits (currency held by treasury), (4) demand deposits, (5) time deposits, (6) foreign exchange deposits, (7) special funds deposits, (8) public debt sinking funds deposits, (9) other deposits, (10) counterpart funds, (11) general government lending funds deposits, (12) capital accounts, and (13) unclassified liabilities.

— *Foreign liabilities*. Included in this category are (1) liabilities to nonresidents mainly involving demand and time deposits in foreign and domestic currency by foreign banks, businesses, and individuals or domestic nationals residing abroad; (2) borrowings from foreign banks, businesses, and individuals; (3) bilateral payment agreements liabilities; (4) payment arrears; (5) import bills payable; (6) debentures issued abroad; (7) other liabilities to nonresidents; (8) offset to own currency circulating abroad.

— *Claims on nonmonetary units*. In the financial and nonfinancial areas, these include several types of instruments, mainly involving (1) loans and advances, (2) bills, (3) rediscounts, (4) treasury bills, (5) government securities, (6) bank investments (shares, bonds, participations), (7) mortgages, (8) overdrafts, and (9) other types of claims in domestic currency on domestic residents.

— *Other assets of monetary institutions*. These mainly include (1) fixed assets, (2) temporary accounts, (3) participation in international financial institutions, (4) nonmonetary precious metals,

(5) subsidiary accounts checks for collection and prepayments, (6) receivables, (7) claims on other deposit money banks (deposits and loans/bonds), and (8) other assets.

— *Foreign assets*. Included in this group are (1) gold, convertible foreign exchange, nonconvertible foreign exchange, treasury foreign assets, and other official foreign assets; (2) loans and advances to nonresident banks and nonbanks; (3) investments in foreign bonds and participation; (4) regional monetary cooperation funds; (5) checks and other types of foreign assets.

— *Other assets/liabilities (net)*. This represents the net amount of "other" assets and liabilities of the central banking system (monetary authorities), other monetary institutions, and the whole monetary system.

THE MATRIX OF FLOW-OF-FUNDS ACCOUNTS

The application of the above classification of transactions by institutional sectors and types of transactions can be used in a flow-of-funds matrix to form a methodological and statistical basis for comparative analysis.

Statistical information found in the *International Financial Statistics* (IFS) (International Monetary Fund) can be presented in a matrix of flow-of-funds accounts. The three groups of data appearing in the IFS report form the basis for compilation of this matrix: (1) static (stock) concept from data on monetary institutions, coded by 10 to 39; (2) dynamic (flow) concept for data on government finance, coded by 80 to 89; (3) dynamic concept for data on balance-of-payments transactions, coded by 77 to 79. Balance-of-payments data are transferred into domestic currency amounts by using the average exchange rate in the period under consideration to express the ratio of domestic currency to one U.S. dollar (coded by "rf"or "rh" in the IFS or by comparable exchange rates if the "rf" or "rh" exchange rates are not available).

This matrix of flow-of-funds accounts appears rather simplified in its classification of economic units by institutional sectors and the classification of transactions by type. Consequently, it is inappropriate for a complex comparative financial analysis that involves monetary and nonmonetary financial transactions and nonfinancial transactions. This matrix is very suitable for a comparative analysis of the MSP, as defined in the model of this analysis. Any difficulties arise when analysis of ratios of monetary transactions to nonmonetary financial transactions and assets and liabilities are included. These ratios can be replaced by ratios to GNP, although this reveals a bias for lower ratios in developing countries and higher ratios in developed economies that have significantly higher ratios of financial transactions, assets, and liabilities to GNP.

NOTES

1. The *Yearbook of National Accounts of the United Nations* provides comparative statistical information on transactions involved in a comparative study of the MSP. The *Financial Statistics of the Organization for Economic Cooperation and Development* (OECD) and *Financial Accounts of OECD Countries* include statistical information on OECD member countries only.

2. Quotations and definitions used in this chapter are taken from the introduction and "A Guide to Money and Banking Statistics in IFS," *International Financial Statistics* (International Monetary Fund, 1984).

5

Empirical Evidence

This chapter will present empirical evidence on the MSP in different types of economies in order to test the hypothesis on the role of the institutional economic system and economic development level.

The hypothesis, which is based on the role of the institutional economic system and level of economic development in the MSP, is defined by a concept, model, and method of empirical analysis. Finally, the results of the empirical analysis are presented, along with conclusions on (1) the consistency of the hypothesis on the role of institutional economic systems; (2) the level of economic development and other determinants in the MSP; (3) the results of empirical evidence showing a comparative analysis of the structure of reserve money creation, the size of monetary multipliers, and the ratios determining monetary multipliers; (4) the role of institutional sectors in the MSP in the central banking system (monetary authorities), other monetary institutions, the central government, other domestic nonmonetary institutional sectors, and the rest of the world's balance of payments; and (5) the interaction of controlled and autonomous transactions in different types of economies in this study.

THE HYPOTHESIS

The hypothesis on the institutional economic system and economic development level needs to define their influence as endogenous factors determining the MSP. Then, the empirical evidence is to be used not only to test this hypothesis but to form final conclusions about the impact of these endogenous and exogenous influences on the MSP. Based on earlier explanations, one of the main assumptions of this hypothesis is that the MSP represents only part of a far broader monetary structure and other financial and nonfinancial transactions and decisionmaking in the portfolio selection behavior of economic units to reach an optimal level in a financial structure and nonfinancial assets. Within this framework, it is supposed that the MSP involves not only variables and changes directly related to money supply changes and other monetary aggregates but also variables and changes involved in financial intermediation and other financial and nonfinancial transactions, domestic and foreign. Focusing on the broad concept of the MSP, the basic thrust of this hypothesis is that the MSP is primarily influenced by the institutional structure of the economic system and the economic development level of an economy. However, it is also assumed that some exogenous influences outside the institutional structure of the economic system and economic development level may have a significant influence on the MSP.

In a methodological approach, it may be assumed that direct and indirect influences on the MSP will be exerted through (1) interrelationships among the variables involved; (2) "carryovers" and their influence on the MSP from the previous period to the next one; and (3) extraordinary economic developments, domestic and foreign. While these influences are not included in this hypothesis, giving the appearance of oversimplification, this is done to avoid a complicated presentation of the hypothesis. That the analysis of these influences is to be the target of empirical analysis is understood.

Monetary Multipliers

Based on this approach, the hypothesis on monetary multipliers is to be investigated empirically. It may be assumed that the level of economic development may logically lead to the following.

1. There is lower leakage of money to nonmonetary deposits (t) at the lower level of economic development because of a lower savings ratio by nonmonetary units, mainly households, interested in these deposits. The opposite may occur because there are more deposits with monetary institutions in total financial investments of nonmonetary units; however, the effects of a low savings ratio may prevail. The higher savings ratio of nonmonetary units at a higher level of economic development is supposed to lead to greater leakage of money to nonmonetary deposits of monetary institutions (t), which happens despite the greater possibil-

ities for financial investments in other types of financial instruments issued by nonmonetary institutions in these economies.

2. Greater leakage of money (lower creation of money) by foreign exchange transactions of monetary institutions (f) should be assumed at a lower level of economic development from a less favorable current account of balance of payments than in developed economies—usually deficit or relatively lower surplus than in developed economies. Greater leakage of money in developing economies should be assumed because of greater involvement by monetary institutions in foreign financial transactions.

3. In this way, ratio $k = 1 - t + f$ reflects two opposite influences on the level of economic development. Within the narrow limits of a balance-of-payments deficit, it is logical to assume that, because of the predominant influence of leakage of money into nonmonetary deposits of monetary institutions (t), a lower ratio k would result in developed economies rather than in developing economies.

4. The entropy ratio of reserve money (e) should be assumed to be greater in developing than in developed economies because of the greater liquidity risk and greater demand for liquid reserve money by monetary institutions under inefficient money market conditions. Greater entropy of reserve money in developing economies also reflects greater reserve requirement ratios from an assumed greater use of this instrument of monetary regulation.

5. Leakage of reserve money into currency in circulation appears logically greater in developing economies from a greater use of currency for payments by households and enterprises. Greater leakage of reserve money into currency in circulation reflects not only a greater demand for currency for current transactions but also increased demand for this currency as a part of assets or store of value.

6. When there is leakage of reserve money into monetary and nonmonetary deposits with the central bank, it is assumed to be greater in developing economies rather than developed economies because of the use of obligatory deposits as an instrument of monetary policy with the central bank. This is a result of an involvement by central banks in the commercial transactions of some of these economies and holding of demand deposits.

7. Total entropy and leakage of reserve money (ratio p) is assumed to be significantly higher in developing rather than developed economies. This results from the combined forces of entropy and leakage of reserve money flows.

8. The size of monetary multipliers at different levels of economic development should be hypothesized. With the opposite influence of ratios k and p on monetary multiplier ($m = k{:}p$) and both ratios being greater in developing economies than in developed economies, the hypothesis on the size of monetary multipliers is developed in comparison with those in developed economies and depends on the higher ratios of p and k in developing economies. The combined effects of the determinants of ratios k and p suggest that ratio p is relatively greater in developing economies than ratio k in comparison with these ratios in developed economies, so that monetary multiplier (m) in developing economies is logically assumed to be lower than in developed economies. However, this hypothesis becomes less clear on the economic development level. With the possible varieties of ratios influencing ratio k and ratio p in developing economies at different levels of economic development, the hypothesis that the monetary multiplier in developed economies is presumably higher than in developing economies does not necessarily mean that monetary multipliers in economies at a higher level of economic development are greater than those at lower levels of economic development.

Institutional Structure of the Economic System

In order to define the hypothesis, the influence of the institutional structure of the economic system on monetary multipliers is considered an indicator of the degree of decentralization and freedom in economic decisionmaking as institutionally determined. In this light, the following hypothesis appears logical:

1. Greater leakage of money into nonmonetary deposits (t) appears more logical in capitalist economies than in socialist economies. It is also more logical to expect a greater leakage of money in the decentralized economic decisionmaking of socialist economies than in socialist centralized economies. Both hypotheses are based on the assumption that at a higher level of decentralization of economic decisionmaking, there exists greater asymmetric savings and investments by the individual economic units, which leads to a greater number of depositors and amounts deposited with monetary institutions.

2. Greater control of leakage or the creation of money by foreign exchange transactions by monetary institutions (f) is logical in socialist economies, particularly in socialist economies with centralized economic decisionmaking. However, more freedom for monetary institutions and involvement by nonmonetary units can be assumed in capitalist econo-

mies. Finally, the direction and size of these effects are predominantly dependent on the balance-of-payments transactions (surplus/deficit of current account). Therefore, the leakage or creation of money by foreign exchange transactions of monetary institutions is primarily the result of economic policy targets, balance-of-payments transactions, and the economic system allowing any size and direction for these flows.

3. Therefore, the hypothesis on the influence of the economic system on total leakage of money and ratio $k = 1 - t + f$ can be based primarily on its influence on leakage of money into nonmonetary deposits with monetary institutions because at the higher degree of decentralization of economic decisionmaking, greater leakage of money and lower ratio k are logical. Thus, lower k is logical in capitalist economies rather than in socialist economies, and lower k is more logical in socialist economies with decentralized decisionmaking than in centralized economic decisionmaking economies.

4. The influence of the institutional economic system on entropy of reserve money (e) can be assumed to be an indirect influence: the higher the degree of decentralization of economic decisionmaking, the stronger the influence of economic development on the entropy of reserve money. Therefore, the level of economic development may have greater influence on entropy of reserve money in economies with a higher degree of economic decentralization, which is greater in capitalist economies than in socialist economies, and greater in socialist decentralized economies than in socialist centralized economies.

5. A similar hypothesis is valid for the influence of the institutional economic system on leakage of reserve money into currency in circulation. However, regulations on the use of currency may have a significant influence, for in socialist economies, there are regulations excluding the use of currency by socialist enterprises as a means of payment, except in payments to private subjects. This may lead to a relatively lower leakage of reserve money into currency in circulation.

6. The influence of the institutional economic system on leakage of reserve money into deposits with the central banks depends on the regulations. The usual regulations eliminating these deposits from central bank transactions in developed capitalist economies is logically reflected in the low deposits with central banks, except central government deposits. The share of these deposits in other capitalist economies is lower than that of socialist decentralized economies, which is lower than in socialist centralized economies. In addition, the greater degree of decentralization of economic decisionmaking provides better conditions for influence at the economic development level.

7. Because of this, there is no logical basis for a hypothesis on the direct influence of the economic system on entropy and leakage of reserve money. The more important hypothesis is that economic systems with a higher degree of decentralization and freedom in economic decisionmaking show a greater influence of the economic development level on entropy and leakage of reserve money, indirectly influencing these reserve money flows.

8. The influence of the economic system on ratios of entropy and leakage of reserve money and money supply in determining monetary multipliers does not clearly indicate its direct influence on monetary multipliers. However, it does indicate the significant indirect influence on monetary multipliers by creating less or more favorable conditions for the influence of the economic development level, relevant economic relationships, and results on these multipliers.

The above hypothesis on both the influence of the institutional economic systems and level of economic development on monetary multipliers assumes the nonsignificant influences of the exogenous determinants of the MSP or those influences emerging from sources other than the institutional economic system and level of economic development. As a result, a hypothesis of possible significant deviations from the above assumed ratios has to be considered, especially on exogenous influences on the MSP.

HYPOTHESIS: CREATION OF RESERVE MONEY STRUCTURE

The Level of Economic Development

The hypothesis on the structure of reserve money creation involves the level of economic development, which may be assumed to have an impact on the creation of reserve money structure in this manner:

1. Less favorable balance-of-payments transactions of economies at the lower level of economic development and their greater sensitivity to the deterioration of foreign markets may be expected to lead to a withdrawal of reserve money by foreign exchange transactions by central banks or to significantly less money created by developing economies than by developed ones. This may be fairly obvious in the period under consideration because of the second increase in oil prices and deteriorating foreign markets. In developed economies, assuming a usually positive current account of balance-of-payments transactions, as much

as central banks are involved in foreign financial transactions, a greater share of creation of reserve money by foreign transactions should be logically expected.

2. Within domestic instruments of creation of reserve money, the traditional central government crediting by central banks ($_cA_g$) should be expected in both developed and developing economies as the most important source for reserve money creation. This is achieved mainly from buying central government securities in developed economies or central bank credits to central governments in developing economies, which have far less efficient financial markets. Thus, no significant difference in the share of central government financing by central banks in reserve money creation and on the economic development level should be expected.

3. Creation of reserve money by central bank crediting of other monetary institutions ($_cA_m$) should be relatively greater in developing economies because of less efficient financial markets, lower supply of deposits by nonmonetary units, and low creation or withdrawal of reserve money by the foreign exchange transactions of these institutions.

4. Creation of reserve money by central bank crediting of nonmonetary units, mainly enterprises, is logically more significant in developing economies; it is rather rare in developed economies with their more sophisticated financial organizations. However, this source for reserve money creation should be less significant than central bank crediting of other monetary institutions in developing economies.

5. Creation of reserve money by extraordinary central bank transactions ($_cU_a$) should be greater in developing economies, assuming there exists a greater need for these transactions in these economies, especially when both foreign and domestic conditions have deteriorated, imposing the need for extraordinary central government intervention.

Influences: Institutional Economic System

No significant direct influence by the institutional economic system on the structure of reserve money creation is to be expected in decentralized economic decisionmaking. However, its indirect influence may be significant in institutional economic systems involving greater government economic intervention and less decentralization and freedom in economic decisionmaking, especially in socialist centralized economies.

1. The share of reserve money creation by foreign transactions means that stronger government control of balance-of-payments transactions in socialist economies may diminish the impact of foreign transactions by

comparison with capitalist economies. Their influence may extend to socialist economies where centralized economic decisionmaking is presumed lower than in socialist economies with decentralized economic decisionmaking.

2. Similar logic can be applied to reserve money creation by domestic instruments. In the creation of reserve money by central bank crediting of the central government, it is logical to expect a similar share of this instrument of reserve money creation in capitalist economies and socialist economies with decentralized economic decisionmaking. Creation of reserve money by this instrument in socialist economies with centralized economic decisionmaking should necessarily be far lower, especially considering the great financial power of the central government, with little need for it to use central bank credits.

3. A similar share of creation of reserve money by central bank crediting of other monetary institutions ($_cA_m$) and central bank crediting of nonmonetary subjects ($_cA_n$) is logical in capitalist economies and socialist economies with decentralized economic decisionmaking. In socialist economies with a centralized economic decisionmaking share of these instruments in the creation of reserve money, it is rather specific. The monobanking system dominates these economies, mainly the central banking system, and the creation of reserve money by the central banking system credits is the same as creation of money by total credits of monetary institutions in economies with decentralized banking systems. In this way, the creation of the reserve money structure in socialist centralized economies is not comparable with that of economies with a decentralized banking system of capitalist economies and socialist economies with decentralized economic decisionmaking.

4. Creation of reserve money by extraordinary central bank transactions ($_cU_a$) is expected to be more active in socialist economies, of course, assuming greater central government and central bank power and responsibility to perform extraordinary intervention, if necessary.

Exogenous Influences

Like the money multipliers, the exogenous influences on the MSP—other than the institutional economic system and the level of economic development, and deterioration of balance of payments in developing economies—are expected to have a similar effect.

The hypothesis on the role of the central banking system and controllability of the MSP is not presented here, nor is a hypothesis defined on the role of other monetary institutions and nonmonetary subjects. We present only hypotheses that can be tested empirically and serve as a basis for the empirical analysis of the MSP. However, the empirical evidence on the role of these institutional sectors is missing, with the role of an institutional sector defined as its source for power in the MSP. As a result, the analysis of the role of these institutional sectors and the degree of controllability of the MSP are presented after an empirical analysis based on a logical interpretation of the issues involved.

THE METHODOLOGICAL APPROACH

Our investigation aims to test the hypothesis on the role of the institutional economic system and economic development level as endogenous determinants, along with the role of other exogenous and endogenous influences contributing to differences in the MSP and empirical analysis. Such investigation should involve: (1) empirical evidence on the size and dispersion of monetary multipliers and their relevant ratios and (2) the creation of a reserve money structure by groups of economies classified by institutional economic system and economic development level. As a result, conclusions on the consistency of the above hypothesis may be presented.

This investigation has to involve both static (stock) approach and dynamic (flow) approach. The static approach includes an analysis of the MSP at the end of 1978 and 1983, while the dynamic approach concerns an analysis of the MSP from 1979 to 1983. In this way, the static approach to a comparative analysis of the MSP explains (1) monetary multipliers and (2) their relevant ratios and creation of reserve money structure, beginning and ending with the empirical evidence. The dynamic approach explains how changes in variables and their relevant ratios were performed in late 1978 and 1983.

Holistic and Structural Comparative Analysis of the MSP

A comparative analysis first includes the holistic analysis of the MSP. This includes an analysis of monetary multipliers, their relevant ratios, and the structure of reserve money creation in economies classified in individual cells of the above classification of economies matrix (with the same institutional system and same level of economic development). A structural comparative analysis then includes a comparative analysis of monetary multipliers, their ratios, and the reserve money creation structure in economies classified in the different cells. Then, conclusions are presented on (1) the role of the institutional system, (2) economic development level, and (3) the influence of exogenous determinants presenting evidence on the MSP contradictory to the hypothesis. Structural analysis should be used for a definition of the final conclusions of comparative analysis of the MSP in representing the target area for this study.

Holistic analysis should provide structural analysis information on (1) central tendencies, (2) dispersion (homogeneity), (3) specific influences by exogenous determinants on dispersion of monetary multipliers with their relevant ratios, and (4) reserve money creation structure within individual groups of economies.

First, the holistic analysis calculates multipliers and relevant ratios for each economy involved in an analysis of the MSP. The second step is to classify economies by the above matrix of classification and introduction of relevant calculated variables and multipliers and ratios for each economy in the appropriate matrix cell. The third step is to calculate the arithmetic means for multipliers and ratios and the measures of the dispersion of variables and ratios involved. The fourth step is to interpret measures of dispersion of the creation of reserve money structure and monetary multipliers, especially those very high or low multipliers, using the above three groups of ratios.

Conclusions may be made about what causes these deviations in the reserve money creation structure, the monetary multipliers of the individual economies involved in a group of economies, and the arithmetic means valid for the whole group of economies, which corresponds to the needs of their use in structural comparative analysis.

Structural comparative analysis of the MSP is designed to investigate the MSP in different types of economies and to present the final conclusions of a comparative analysis of the MSP. Thus, while holistic analysis assumes the insignificant differences in the MSP in the same type economy with explanations of any differences, the structural comparative analysis assumes significant differences in the MSP in the different types of economies. It is designed to investigate whether they prove or disprove the hypothesis on the role of the institutional economic system and the level of economic development in the MSP.

In this way, the structural comparative analysis investigates whether all of the components of the MSP in the different types of economies are consistent with the hypothesis of the role of the institutional economic system and the level of economic development in the MSP. This begins by explaining the differences in the creation of reserve money structure and monetary multiplication by groups of economies on the relevant ratios comprising a consistent or inconsistent creation of money structure and monetary multiplication with the hypothesis explaining these variations in the compound, basic, and explanatory ratios of the hypothesis. The result should be a correct hypothesis on the role of the institutional economic system and the level of economic development in the MSP, parallel with a conclusion on the role of exogenous variables outside the economic system and the level of economic development in the MSP. An example would be a significant contradiction between the evidence on the creation of reserve money structure, monetary multipliers, and relevant ratios and the hypothesis on the role of the economic system and the level of economic development in the MSP.

The first step in this analysis is to prepare a comparative presentation of monetary multipliers and relevant ratios in the above matrix classification of economies, including arithmetic means prepared and analyzed within the holistic analysis of the MSP. The presentation of monetary multipliers and relevant ratios is undertaken to make possible comparisons by economic systems (horizontally), by the level of economic development (vertically), and by both economic systems and the level of economic development (cross comparison). For each ratio presented in this way, a more detailed explanation showing greater differences between the hypothesis and the empirical evidence in the holistic analysis should be explained.

The second step in structural comparative analysis is to examine the consistency of the hypothesis on the role of the institutional economic system and the level of economic development in the MSP with the empirical evidence.

The third step involves an explanation of (1) the differences between the hypothesis on the role of the institutional economic system and the level of economic development in the MSP; (2) the evidence on the structure of creation of reserve money; and (3) monetary multipliers and their relevant ratios by groups of economies classified in the above matrix of classification. In addition to conclusions presented in the holistic analysis, this explanation has to amplify the differences in monetary multipliers by using compound ratios, with an explanation of compound ratios by basic ratios, and, if necessary, an explanation of the basic ratios by partial ratios that indicate significant sources of exogenous influences possibly contributing to an explanation of the differences between hypothesized and actual size and distribution of monetary multipliers and their relevant ratios by groups of economies.

Specific Features of Comparative Analysis of the MSP

In order to avoid confusion about the empirical evidence, we should discuss some aspects of a comparative investigation of the MSP with the limitation this evidence imposes.

1. The exogenous influences on the MSP may be rather different, interacting and affecting the MSP in dissimilar economies and groups of economies in different ways. These effects impact on the MSP in balance-of-payments transactions[1] in foreign financial transactions, production structure, history, heritage and ideology, the size of the country, stability of the system, and natural environment. These influences on the MSP may be especially strong in economies at the lower level of economic development.

2. We should consider the direct effect on the MSP by endogenous and exogenous sources, because their interaction may provide clues as to the origins of the influences on the MSP, especially in countries at a lower level of economic development. An example is the impact at the lower level of economic development on the lower differentiation and efficiency of financial organizations.

3. Empirical evidence may be strongly influenced by differences within the same institutional economic system in socialist economies involving a small number of economies of this type that logically increase the probability of relatively greater differences among the economies involved. The same is valid for groups of economies classified within a level of economic development according to per capita GNP: (1) the groups of economies include economies with rather different per capita GNP; and (2) economies at a similar level of per capita GNP may be at a rather different level of economic development as defined in broader terms of degrees of economic efficiency in differentiation of monetary and financial organizations.

4. Significant deviations in the creation of reserve money structure, monetary multipliers, and their relevant ratios are inherited from unadjusted processes from the previous period. For example, the creation of a relatively large amount of reserve money near the end of the previous period leaves insufficient time for an appropriate MSP follow-up. In addition, "unadjusted" processes—creation of a large amount of reserve money close to the end of the period under consideration—may be carried over to the next period.

5. Deviations in the creation of money structure, money multipliers, and their ratios from the hypothesis may come from extraordinary domestic developments and economic policy measures related to these

developments in monetary policy measures. These deviations directly influence the MSP in restrictive or expansive monetary policy and interest rate policy, and foreign exchange policy measures involving regulations on foreign transactions and regulation of exchange rates. Since the second increase in oil prices (1979), and the changes in domestic and international economic developments, this period becomes particularly important.

6. The exogenous influences on the MSP are predominantly biased, with some random components. This means that influential exogenous sources contribute to an illogically greater dispersion of the more complex ratios in comparison with the dispersion of ratios at a lower level of complexity (illogical if only random influences are assumed). This suggests that less complex ratios may help explain the variations in the creation of reserve money structure more efficiently, along with monetary multipliers, and their relevant ratios from the hypothesis than the more complex ratios. In this way, the less complex ratios offer a better explanation of the role of exogenous influences on the MSP than the more complex ratios. The relevant ratios to monetary multipliers fall into three groups: complex, basic, and explanatory in the approach to explain the role of exogenous influences on the MSP. This approach can be facilitated if the economies in a cell of the matrix classification are subclassified by size of monetary multipliers or the structure of reserve money creation. For example, there may be a classification of economies within a cell in economies with monetary multipliers greater than the arithmetic mean of multipliers plus standard deviation, those with multipliers lower than the arithmetic mean minus standard deviation, and in economies with monetary multipliers between these two highs and lows of monetary multipliers.

In addition, variability and dispersion in the creation of reserve money structure, monetary multipliers, and their ratios must be logically greater in dynamic (flow) than in static (stock) considerations, especially in cases where there are greater differences between stock variables and ratios at the end rather than at the beginning of the period under study. However, greater dispersion of flow monetary multipliers, their ratios, and creation of reserve money structure may result in deviations from the logical relationships (above) between their stock and flow values, as reflected in an increase in average stock variables with a lower flow variable or their decrease with a higher flow variable.

The empirical evidence about the hypothesis on the role of the institutional economic system and economic development level should not be oversimplified. A test of the hypothesis on the role of the

institutional economic system and economic development level as determinants of the MSP should involve a flexible approach. This would allow
significant deviations in empirical results from this hypothesis caused by
several exogenous groups on the MSP and from the institutional system
and the economic development level without necessarily disproving the
hypothesis. The rigid interpretation of the empirical evidence on the
hypothesis of the role of the institutional economic system and economic
development level would mean the false assumption that economies
classified in individual cells of the matrix classification are perfectly
homogeneous and that there are no exogenous influences, including
random ones, on this complex MSP structure. This might lead to false
conclusions about (1) the influence of the institutional economic system,
(2) economic development level, and (3) the empirical evidence from the
hypothesis.

This means that the case for consistent empirical evidence in the
hypothesis on the role of the institutional economic system and economic
development level can be interpreted as the proof that the hypothesis is
correct: exogenous variables do not significantly distort the influence of
the economic system and economic development level on the MSP or
that they do not exist. To explain, a significant deviation of multipliers
and relevant ratios from the hypothesis, based on endogenous variables
and their large dispersion, is the result of an intense distorted influence
by exogenous variables. These variables cause deviations in the empirical
evidence from the hypothesis that do not necessarily mean the hypothesis
is false. According to the Lakatos theory,[2] this may mean that the
empirical evidence shows that to assume that the role of exogenous
variables is not significant is wrong, not necessarily meaning that the
hypothesis on the role of the economic system and economic development
level in the MSP is false. Our approach, using ratios at three levels of
complexity for a multilevel analysis of multipliers and relevant ratios,
should give an insight and more reliable basis for conclusions about the
endogenous and exogenous variable structure in the MSP in individual
types of economies, as classified by economic system and economic
development level.

THE BASIC STRUCTURE OF THE MODEL

The model of comparative empirical analysis of the MSP is to be based
on the beginning formula presenting the MSP:

$$M = {}_cA \cdot m$$

Based on this beginning formula, the model of comparative empirical analysis of the MSP includes two parts that include two groups of questions, variables, and ratios:

c_A = variables and ratios explaining the creation of reserve money

m = variables and ratios explaining the multiplication of the reserve money process

We explain c_A by using a ratio presenting the share of basic types of creation of reserve money in total amounts of creation of money:

$$a_d + a_g + a_n + a_m + a_u + a_f = 1$$

$$a_d = c_{Ad}:c_A$$
$$a_g = c_{Ag}:c_A$$
$$a_n = c_{An}:c_A$$
$$a_m = c_{Am}:c_A$$
$$a_u = c_{Ua}:c_A$$
$$a_f = c_{En}:c_A$$

Multiplier m is explained by three types of ratios: complex ratios, basic ratios, and explanatory ratios.

Complex ratios are

$$k = 1 - t + f$$

and

$$p = e + c + d + c_t$$

Using these two complex ratios, the monetary multiplier is defined by:

$$m = k:p$$

The basic ratios focus on explaining the complex ratios. There are two basic ratios explaining complex ratio k and four basic ratios explaining compound ratio p:

The basic ratios explaining complex ratio k are:

$$t = T{:}A \quad \text{and} \quad f = E_n{:}A$$

The basic ratios explaining complex ratio p are:

$$
\begin{aligned}
e &= R{:}A \\
c &= C{:}A \\
d &= {}_cDM{:}A \\
{}_ct &= {}_cT{:}A
\end{aligned}
$$

The explanatory ratios explain the two basic ratios, t and $_ct$:

$$t = t_q + t_u, \quad \text{where}$$

$$
\begin{aligned}
t_q &= QM{:}A \\
t_u &= U_e{:}A
\end{aligned}
$$

and

$$_ct = {}_ct_q + {}_ct_u, \quad \text{where}$$

$$
\begin{aligned}
{}_ct_q &= {}_cQM{:}A \\
{}_ct_u &= {}_cU_e{:}A
\end{aligned}
$$

Observe that the above model of comparative analysis of the MSP does not involve econometric equations. The main reason for this is the matrix approach to this comparative analysis, which involves a two-dimensional classification of economies. So far, there is no method to calculate the matrix and vector variables in economics as one can, for example, in physics, or to use graphic presentations of these variables and their relationships. Consequently, the only way to interpret matrix and vector variables and ratios in economics is by verbal explanation of their relationships.

The comparative analysis of the MSP in this book is based on the total population of countries with their presentation on the country pages of *International Financial Statistics*. This excludes countries with a population of less than two million and those countries without relevant statistical information for the period under consideration. The total population basis for this study should be meaningful for a statistical measurement and interpretation of the variables and ratios involved and conclusions based on this analysis.

NOTES

1. Some inconsistencies in statistical information on balance-of-payments transactions in *International Financial Statistics* may be relevant for the role of these transactions in the MSP. (See *International Monetary Fund*, "Report on the World Current Account Discrepancy," 1987.)

2. Imre Lakatos, *The Methodology of Scientific Research Programs, and Mathematics, Science and Epistemology* (New York: Cambridge University Press, 1978).

6

Holistic Analysis of the Money
Supply Process

The holistic analysis is designed to explain the basic characteristics of the MSP in countries with the same institutional economic system and level of economic development.

Three approaches to this interpretation of the MSP are used: (1) the "static" approach explains the structure and dispersion of relevant ratios at the end of 1978 and 1983, which are based on portfolio choice considerations; (2) the "dynamic" approach reveals the changes in money supply and relevant ratios from flows registered during 1979 to 1983; (3) the "functional" approach focuses on the structure, dispersion, and changes in the relevant ratios and flows emanating from the particular type of institutional economic system, level of economic development, and other significant influences on the MSP. An assessment with supporting empirical evidence should be included with the hypothesis on the role of this type of economic system, its consistency, and level of economic development within the MSP.

After this approach, a holistic analysis of the MSP for each cell of the matrix includes (1) an explanation of the size and dispersion of monetary multipliers, relevant ratios, and creation of reserve money flows and structure in late 1978 and 1983; (2) an interpretation of the increase in money supply and monetary multiplication, and changes in the structure of reserve money creation from 1979 to 1983, with ratios determining changes in monetary multipliers; and (3) conclusions related to a structural comparative analysis. This includes an assessment of the consistency of the hypothesis on the role of the institutional economic system and economic development level in the MSP and offers empirical evidence with an explanation of the significant differences between the hypothesis and the empirical evidence presented. An interpretation should follow of size variations in monetary multipliers, leakages of money (ratio k), leakages and entropy of reserve money (ratio p), and variation in both ratios.

In addition, we should determine which ratios contribute to variations in the size of the above complex ratios and which explanatory ratios contribute to these variations in the basic ratios that will, we hope, lead to some conclusions about the origins of the variations in monetary multipliers in a classification group of economies. This would include size of the share of some reserve money sources, especially those under exogenous influences.

INDUSTRIAL ECONOMIES

The countries included in this group are at the highest level of economic development with a per capita GNP of more than $4,600, highly developed and diverse free markets, financial institutions and instruments, and flow.

The MSP in these countries is characterized by (1) a relatively high average monetary multiplier (arithmetic mean) that varies greatly in the individual countries; and (2) a decrease in monetary multipliers in nearly all of the economies involved, with the average increase in money adjusting downward to 49 percent in 1979 to 1983. This was the result of a larger increase in reserve money creation (88 percent) than in monetary multiplication—the monetary multiplier was 14 percent lower in late 1983 than in late 1978. The similar rate of increase in money supply and the nominal GNP and stable income velocity of money in circulation in this period shows an increase in reserve money creation that adjusted to the decrease in monetary multipliers to pursue a policy of monetary equilibrium for the whole group of countries.

The relatively high average monetary multiplier in these economies is fully consistent with the hypothesis on the role of the economic system and the economic development level of monetary multipliers. However, this conclusion is weakened by the wide range of differences in monetary multipliers for individual countries. For example, in table 6.1, if the standard deviation in monetary multipliers were increased by 83 percent, parallel with the decrease in the average multiplier (compare late 1983 and 1978), the coefficient of relative dispersion (standard deviation divided by the arithmetic mean) reached at the end of 1983 was 0.49, or

Table 6.1
Monetary Multipliers and Basic Monetary Ratios of Industrial Countries

	Monetary Multi-pliers			Leakage of Money Supply k			Leakage and Entropy of Reserve Money p		
	End 1978	1979–83	End 1983	End 1978	1979–83	End 1983	End 1978	1978–83	End 1983
Arith-metic mean	1.82	1.46	1.56	0.34	0.19	0.27	0.20	0.21	0.20
Standard devi-ation	0.56	1.49	0.77	0.08	0.11	0.12	0.08	0.19	0.11
Range	2.34	6.40	2.11	0.38	0.50	0.42	0.41	0.57	0.38
Relative Standard Deviation	0.31	1.02	0.99	0.24	0.58	0.44	0.40	0.90	0.55
Relative Range	1.29	4.38	1.35	1.12	2.63	1.56	2.05	2.78	1.90

Source: International Financial Statistics.

49 percent below and over the arithmetic mean, or 58 percent more than at the end of 1978. This would be the result of a 3.3 times greater relative standard deviation in 1979 to 1983 (flow consideration) than at the end of 1978. Similar changes are not observed in relative range (range divided by arithmetic mean) that remained nearly stable in stock (late 1983 compared with late 1978), although 3.4 times greater in flow considerations.

Closer examination reveals that in complex ratios k and p, the leading cause of an increased dispersion of monetary multipliers reflects the increased dispersion of complex ratio k (leakage of money supply). This includes leakage of money to nonmonetary deposits (t) and the effects of foreign exchange transactions on monetary institutions through changes in foreign assets and liabilities of these institutions, E_n. The relative standard deviation in this ratio k was significantly higher than the monetary multipliers, 83 percent greater in late 1983 than at the end of 1978. The relative standard deviation of the other complex ratio determining monetary multiplier (p), which reflects entropy and leakage of reserve money, was only 38 percent greater than the monetary multiplier.

Evidence that the increased dispersion of the monetary multiplier stems from an increased dispersion of the ratio k leads one to conclude that foreign exchange transactions of monetary institutions are the basic source for the increase in dispersion of monetary multipliers. This is logical under the existing deterioration in foreign markets, especially financial markets after the second increase in oil prices. These factors impacted in different ways on the transactions of the individual economies, generating the principle causes of increased dispersion of the ratio k, and dispersion of monetary multipliers of the individual economies. This process is logical if the significant differences in efficiency and differentiation in the financial organization of the economies involved are considered.

The relatively high average monetary multiplier of this group of countries reflects the logical but expected influence of the highest level of economic development in these free market economies with an accompanying differentiated and efficient monetary and financial organization. The relatively high degree of dispersion of monetary multipliers by individual economies is the result of significant differences in the level of economic development among these economies. This process was accompanied by differentiation and efficiency in the monetary and financial organization that was further strengthened by the impact of a deterioration in foreign and domestic economic development in the MSP of the individual economies after the second increase in oil prices in 1979.

For a closer look at the differences in the monetary multipliers of the individual economies, a classification of economies in this group based on size of multipliers may be helpful. For example, if five countries with the lowest monetary multipliers of less than 1.00 are compared with five countries with the highest monetary multipliers of greater than 2.00,[1] it appears that (1) differences in the size of these monetary multipliers in the two subgroups reflect a significantly larger p ratio in the first than in the second subgroup of countries; and (2) the higher p ratio in the first group reflects greater central bank involvement in extraordinary financial interventions (ratio ct), which appears to be a logical process for economies at the lower level of financial differentiation under conditions imposed by the second increase in oil prices (table 6.2).

The complex ratio p, which appears mainly related to differentiation and the function of monetary and other financial institutions, determines primarily the size of monetary multipliers. While strongly influenced by

Table 6.2
Industrial Economies with the Lowest and Highest Monetary Multipliers
(Ending 1983)

Arithmetic means of:	Economies with multipliers lower than 1.00	Economies with multipliers greater than 2.00	All economies involved
Monetary Multipliers	0.85	2.59	1.56
k ratios	0.24	2.26	0.27
p ratios	0.28	0.10	0.20
e ratios	0.04	0.02	0.04
c ratios	0.07	0.06	0.08
$_c t$ ratios	0.16	0.01	0.08

Source: International Financial Statistics.

a deterioration in balance of payments, complex ratio k primarily contributes to the dispersion of monetary multipliers in a climate of significant differences related to the economic development level and the structure of monetary and financial institutions.

In an explanation of the creation of reserve money structure, the framework of financial investments of the central banking system, including net foreign assets, the basic characteristic is a nearly equal creation of reserve money by domestic and foreign exchange transactions. In addition, the average share of domestic and foreign exchange transactions in reserve money creation proves to be fairly stable, although the dispersion of their shares in individual countries is larger than monetary multipliers (table 6.3). This includes countries, e.g., United Kingdom and New Zealand, whose foreign transactions in late 1978 and 1983 represent instruments of withdrawal of reserve money, along with

Table 6.3
Structure of Reserve Money Creation: Industrial Countries (Percentage of Total)

		c^E_n	c^A_d	c^A_g	c^A_n	c^A_m	c^U_a
Arithmetic							
Mean	End 1978	0.46	0.54	0.39	0.05	0.11	0.01
	1979-83	0.43	0.57	0.36	0.04	0.18	0.00
	End 1983	0.46	0.54	0.38	0.04	0.12	0.01
Rela-	End 1978	0.67	0.57	0.79	2.20	0.32	0.25
tive	1979-83	0.70	0.65	1.00	5.20	1.61	-
Standard							
Devi-	End 1983	0.63	0.54	0.79	2.75	1.17	3.00
ation							
Rela-	End 1978	2.70	2.22	2.87	8.20	3.45	8.00
tive	1979-83	2.74	2.32	4.57	17.00	6.61	-
Range	End 1983	1.89	1.61	2.57	12.00	3.42	14.00

Source: International Financial Statistics.

West Germany, Japan, and Canada in 1979 to 1983. However, one country (Australia) created reserve money exclusively through foreign transactions.

Highlighting the creation of reserve money is its relationship with the current account of balance-of-payments transactions. In these countries, the direct interrelationships between balance-of-payments transactions and reserve money creation is weak, which indicates not only a strong position but independent behavior by the central banking systems in these countries in balance-of-payments transactions and involvement of non-monetary entities in foreign financial transactions. Thus, 13 of the 19 countries in this group had current account deficits during 1979 to 1983, with only one country of these 13 involved in the withdrawal of reserve money by foreign exchange transactions. However, only one of the other 6 surplus current account countries experienced a withdrawal of reserve money by foreign exchange transactions.

Similar conclusions appear justified in the reserve money structure in domestic transactions. The main source for the creation of domestic reserve money appears to be the credit instruments of the central government and the credit instruments for other monetary institutions. The relatively large dispersion of the share of these instruments in total reserve money creation by individual economies can be observed, indicating again the impact of differences in the level of economic development, degrees of differentiation, and operations of monetary/financial institutions and markets.

The conclusion on both monetary multipliers and the reserve money creation structure, with the average magnitudes of ratios and percent shares, is that empirical evidence proves the hypothesis on the high level of influence of economic development, differentiation, and efficiency of the monetary and financial organization of these economies on the MSP. The dispersion of ratios and percentage shares by the individual economies indicates a significant impact on the relevant differences in economic development level and differentiation among financial institutions in this group of countries and the effects of strong exogenous influences during this period, especially a deterioration in balance-of-payments transactions following the second increase in oil prices.

OIL-EXPORTING DEVELOPING COUNTRIES

This is a specific group of countries with differences from industrial countries and other developing non–oil-exporting countries. When compared with industrial nations, their successful balance-of-payments transactions make them similar, which signifies a very healthy current account surplus and resulting high per capita GNP from these transactions. Noticeable differences appear in the lower efficiency of the economy and financial structure, with less differentiation and efficiency in the financial institutions and markets and financial instrument structure than in industrial countries. When compared with developing economies, they are similar in low efficiency of the economy and financial structure but different in higher per capita GNP and successful balance-of-payments transactions. A similar MSP with developing economies in the role of the institutional economic system and economic development level may be assumed; however, variations emanating from exogenous influences on the MSP in balance-of-payments transactions should be expected in the surplus current account of these transactions.

Another significant characteristic of these countries is the wide range of differences in per capita GNP, from $450 in countries on the low side of development to more than $28,000, which exceeds the per capita GNP in the most developed industrial countries. The size of the country contributes to the differences in the MSP (population ranges from nearly 1 million to over 156 million).

Beginning with an explanation of monetary developments, the money supply increased like the nominal GNP (107 percent), which allowed the income velocity of money in circulation to remain unchanged. However, the decrease in the monetary multiplier was accompanied by a higher rate of increase in reserve money than money supply (157 percent).

The lower monetary multiplier in these economies appears contradictory when we consider other developing economies with a much higher per capita GNP. The lower monetary multiplier in these economies reconfirms the above rule that a simplified financial structure and no significant financial market role influence the MSP in the same way, regardless of the differences in economic development level as measured by per capita GNP. In addition, a closer look reveals that a lower monetary multiplier in these economies primarily reflects a better balance-of-payments position. The lower monetary multiplier basically results from leakage of reserve money representing central government deposits with the central banks, which originated from high oil export receipts from central governments. The extra high leakage of reserve money, which is represented by the very high p ratio 1.60 at the end of 1983, more than compensated for the large k ratio or low leakage of money reflecting the significant creation of money from foreign exchange transactions by monetary institutions that increased their net foreign assets in a logical progression under the balance-of-payments current account surplus.

Therefore, relatively low monetary multipliers appear in this economic group from opposite influences at play in favorable balance-of-payments transactions because, on one hand, they contribute to greater monetary multipliers as a significant source for money creation or increased k ratio as a result of an increase in the f ratio. On the other hand, they contribute to a lower monetary multiplier by causing accumulation of central government deposits with the central banks or leakage of reserve money. This explains the same decrease in the average stock monetary multiplier under study of 6 percent from a decrease in k ratio of 25 percent and a decrease in the p ratio of 22 percent. This more intense dispersion of the k and p ratios is an integral part of the MSP in this group of economies as it reflects the impact of the balance-of-payments transactions on the MSP (table 6.4).

The best indicator of the different effects of balance-of-payments transactions may be observed by comparing multipliers and their basic ratios in an economy with lower than m $-$ σ and the economy with higher than m $+$ σ (σ = standard deviation of m). This comparison reveals that the great difference in monetary multipliers in these economies, 0.17 in Saudi Arabia and 2.47 in Algeria, is the exclusive result of a p ratio 27 times greater in the first than in the second country, or 9.65 versus 0.36, which compensated for the double impact of k ratio in the first country rather than the second of 1.60 versus 0.89. Both of these differences

Table 6.4
Monetary Multipliers and Basic Monetary Ratios of Oil-Exporting Developing Economies

	Monetary Multipliers			Leakage of Money Supply (k)			Leakage and Entropy of Reserve Money (p)		
	End 1978	1979–83	End 1983	End 1978	1979–83	End 1983	End 1978	1978 83	End 1983
Arithmetic Mean	0.94	1.10	0.89	0.86	0.58	0.65	2.05	1.42	1.60
Standard Deviation	0.31	1.05	0.61	0.93	0.31	0.43	4.17	2.35	2.86
Range	1.71	2.90	2.30	3.17	0.83	1.45	13.58	7.68	9.35
Relative Standard Deviation	0.32	0.95	0.69	1.08	0.53	0.66	2.03	1.65	1.79
Relative Range	1.82	2.64	2.58	3.69	1.43	2.23	6.62	5.41	5.84

Source: International Financial Statistics.

primarily reflect the various effects of balance-of-payments transactions on the MSP.

Foreign exchange transactions remain the most significant source for the creation of reserve money (table 6.5). Within the domestic framework for the creation of reserve money, the central bank credits to the central government remain the main instrument for the creation of this money. The central bank credits share to other monetary institutions increased, while central bank credits share to nonmonetary subjects declined. Extraordinary measures by the central bank are prominent from 1979 to 1983, but at the close of 1983, their share in reserve money creation was relatively low, although logical under the circumstances.

NON–OIL-EXPORTING DEVELOPING CAPITALIST ECONOMIES

Per Capita GNP $830–$4,600

This group is at the highest level of economic development for developing economies as measured by per capita GNP. The wide range

Table 6.5
Reserve Money Creation Structure of Oil-Exporting Developing Economies

		c^E_n	c^A_d	c^A_g	c^A_n	c^A_m	c^U_a
Arithmetic							
Mean	End 1978	0.58	0.92	0.27	0.07	0.08	0.00
	1979-83	0.62	0.38	0.11	0.01	0.12	1.14
	End 1983	0.63	0.37	0.21	0.03	0.11	0.02
Relative	End 1978	0.52	0.72	0.83	2.09	1.20	33.33
Standard	1979-83	0.71	1.17	3.30	2.73	1.74	2.73
Deviation	End 1983	0.55	0.95	1.30	0.97	1.40	2.27
Relative	End 1978	1.40	1.93	2.37	6.87	2.89	10.00
Range	1979-83	1.88	3.11	12.41	9.09	4.70	8.92
	End 1983	1.50	2.59	3.99	6.13	3.36	7.27

Source: International Financial Statistics.

of differences in the economic development levels of the individual economies in this group contributes to the increased dispersion of relationships in the MSP. This lower level of economic development, not found in industrial economies, is accompanied by lower differentiation, and an efficient monetary and financial organization demands greater participation by monetary institutions, especially the central banks, as reflected in the MSP. An important exogenous characteristic of these economies is the increased deficit in the balance-of-payments current account that has a stronger impact on the MSP than would be observed in oil-exporting developing or industrial economies.

The MSP in these economies has a lower average monetary multiplier than would be found in industrial economies; this is consistent with the hypothesis on the influence of the economic development level on the MSP. The MSP exhibits a significant decrease of 15 percent in the average monetary multiplier, which indicates an increase of 341 percent in the money supply from 1979 to 1983.[2] This was accomplished by a greater increase in reserve money creation than in the money supply. There was an increase of 6.84 percent in late 1978 and 7.19 percent in late 1983 in the income velocity of money, which represents the money supply to nominal GNP ratio. This indicates that this rate of increase in reserve money creation may be restrictive.

These conclusions, which are based on average values of ratios and percentage changes in relevant variables, appear to differ in the individual economies because of the various exogenous influences.

Table 6.6
Monetary Multipliers and Basic Monetary Ratios of Non–Oil-Exporting Developing Capitalist Economies ($830–$4,600 Per Capita GNP)

	Monetary Multipliers			Leakage of Money Supply (k)			Leakage and Entropy of Reserve Money (p)		
	End 1978	1979–83	End 1983	End 1978	1979–83	End 1983	End 1978	1978–83	End 1983
Arithmetic Mean	0.92	0.81	0.81	0.45	0.23	0.29	0.55	0.37	0.42
Standard Deviation	0.29	0.58	0.39	0.19	0.14	0.15	0.25	0.21	0.20
Range	1.67	2.84	2.11	0.71	0.51	0.61	1.15	0.75	0.68
Relative Standard Deviation	0.32	0.72	0.48	0.42	0.61	0.52	0.45	0.60	0.48
Relative Range	1.82	3.53	2.59	1.58	2.24	2.10	2.09	2.03	1.62

Source: International Financial Statistics.

Table 6.6 shows that the decrease in the average monetary multiplier in this group of economies resulted from a greater decrease in ratio k, representing the leakage of money, than the decrease in ratio p, representing leakage and entropy of reserve money. This indicates that the deterioration of balance-of-payments transactions after the second oil price increase strongly influenced leakage of money or decrease in net foreign assets (increase in net foreign liabilities of monetary institutions) and partly compensated for (1) lower leakage and entropy of reserve money on accounts of monetary institutions with the central bank, (2) currency in circulation, and (3) deposits of nonmonetary institutions with central banks. Table 6.6 also suggests that the increased dispersion of monetary multipliers was primarily the result of increased dispersion of ratios k and p, which reflect the different effects of exogenous influences.

Additional information about this group of economies indicates wide differences in the monetary multipliers of these economies. These differences reflect the combined effects of greater leakage of money (T, E_m)

contributing to a lower ratio k, and greater leakage and entropy of reserve money contributing to a greater ratio p in economies with the lowest monetary multipliers. The opposite flows of leakage and entropy of money and reserve money, as reflected in a higher ratio k and a lower ratio p, are observable in economies with the highest monetary multipliers.

These differences appear as a logical result of a deterioration in the balance-of-payments transactions, causing increased leakage of money (E_m) in economies with the lowest multipliers and low degree of adjustment by monetary institutions in these economies to the altered circumstances that require more rational behavior.

Change highlights the creation of reserve money structure resulting from a deterioration in balance-of-payments transactions. Although foreign exchange transactions represented a source for the creation of money in late 1978—similar to industrial economies—they became the instrument for withdrawal of money during this period. This indicates a stronger influence of balance-of-payments transactions on reserve money creation than in industrial economies. The creation of reserve money structure by domestic instruments was significantly changed, involving a lower share of central bank credits to nonmonetary subjects, with a sharp increase in the share of extraordinary instruments in the creation of reserve money. However, reserve money creation by central government financing and the financing of monetary institutions by the central banks remain the main sources for reserve money creation.

Per Capita GNP $360–$829

Economies at the lower level of economic development are less differentiated, and inefficiently organized monetarily and financially than the previous group of developing economies. This is reflected in the prominent role of monetary institutions in both domestic and foreign financial transactions, the minor role of nonmonetary financial institutions, and the negligible role of financial markets. A greater sensitivity of balance-of-payments transactions to a deteriorating foreign market is reflected in the effects of the greater sensitivity of monetary institutions to deteriorating balance-of-payments transactions. As a result, greater impact from exogenous influences on the MSP may be expected in these economies.

A decline in the monetary multiplier reveals that the increase in money supply was performed by increasing reserve money at a higher rate than money supply from late 1983 to late 1978. Once again, the increase in income velocity of money circulation (6.14 to 6.93) indicates that restrictive monetary policy can support improvement in balance-of-payments transactions.

Lower monetary multipliers in these economies than in industrial economies proves the hypothesis on the function of economic development in the MSP. The slightly higher monetary multiplier of these economies than those in the previous group again suggests that differences in the level of economic development, as measured by per capita GNP below the level of economic development of industrial economies, are not reflected in the size of the monetary multipliers. The logic of this conclusion is that the differentiation and efficiency of monetary and financial organizations and other monetary multiplication determinants related to the economic development level are similar at different levels of economic development. Great dispersion of monetary multipliers by individual economies in this group is apparent; however, dispersion of monetary multipliers in these economies was decreased contrary to the increased dispersion of multipliers in the previous group of developing economies at a higher level of economic development, as measured by the relative standard deviation in the monetary multipliers of the individual economies.

The slight decrease in the average monetary multiplier of this group of economies reflects a significant decrease in the leakage of money (ratio k), which is accompanied by a relatively lower decrease in the leakage and entropy of reserve money (ratio p).

The decrease in ratio k mainly reflects the effects of a deterioration in balance-of-payments transactions. A decrease in ratio p mainly reflects a decrease in currency being held by the population, which is logical under the economic growth conditions of these less developed economies.

In a comparison of the three economies having the lowest monetary multipliers (equal and less than $m - \sigma$) and three economies having the highest monetary multipliers (greater than $m + \sigma$), it appears that the difference in multipliers of these two groups (0.44 versus 1.72) reflects a significantly lower k ratio and a greater p ratio in the first group. The highest monetary multipliers in the second group primarily reflect rather low leakage and entropy of reserve money (p ratio).

Similar to the first group of these economies in a higher level of economic development, the creation of reserve money has changed significantly because of a deterioration in balance-of-payments transactions, sensitivity to the various monetary institutions, and the MSP in balance-of-payments transactions:

1. Foreign exchange transactions, the instrument for reserve money creation in late 1978, became the instrument to withdraw

reserve money during 1979 to 1983; consequently, in late 1983, they were viewed as the instruments to withdraw 40 percent of the total reserve money created by central banks.

2. The domestic instrument structure in the creation of reserve money as a parallel increase in the share of credits to central governments and nonmonetary subjects is present.

3. The new and indeed extraordinary central bank investments are pronounced, while the share of credits to monetary institutions has experienced a reduction.

Deteriorating balance-of-payments accounts have impacted significantly on the domestic instruments structure in reserve money creation by imposing extraordinary central bank intervention in domestic financing, including the financing of escalating budget deficits of central governments. The sharp rise in the share of domestic instruments in reserve money creation was accompanied by a decline in the relative dispersion of percent shares of these instruments in total reserve money creation in individual countries, as measured by relative standard deviation. This reflects the high degree of homogeneity through the influence of deteriorating balance-of-payments transactions on reserve money creation in these economies. An increase in the relative dispersion of percent shares of credits to monetary and nonmonetary subjects combined with extraordinary central bank interventions reflect the diverse impact of the balance-of-payments transactions on the domestic instruments structure in reserve money creation.

Per Capita GNP Less than $360

This group, which is at the lowest level of economic development, includes capitalist economies within this framework: (1) the least differentiation in their monetary and financial organization, (2) a most prominent role for monetary institutions (central banks, especially) in their financial transactions, (3) large balance-of-payments deficits, and (4) acute sensitivity of monetary institutions to foreign transactions. The decline in foreign markets and the second increase in oil prices impacted profoundly on the MSP.

The increase in money supply in these economies from 1979 to 1983 (139 percent on an average) was nearly the same as the nominal increase in the GNP, which did not significantly change the income velocity of this money. However, the increase in the money supply, as in other developing economies, was more the result of expanded reserve money creation (186 percent), while the average monetary multiplier decreased by 5 percent between late 1978 and 1983.

The appearance of a slightly higher monetary multiplier in these economies than in other developing economies proves once again the conclusion that the differences in the economic development level within developing economies do not significantly determine monetary multipliers or that a decreasing order of economic development should not necessarily be accompanied by a decreasing order of the monetary multiplier. In other developing economies during this period, the monetary multiplier experienced a decline because of a decrease in ratio k, the result of deteriorating current account balance of payments. A parallel lower decrease in ratio p partly compensates for the increased leakage of money (ratio k). A decrease in ratio p primarily reflects a decrease in currency held by the population—a logical process in economic development. However, the size of the currency holdings of the population in this study remained the highest among all groups of economies, since the countries in this group are at the lowest level of economic development.

The increased dispersion of k ratios suggests the varied impact of a deterioration in balance-of-payments transactions, while a decline in the dispersion of p ratios is the result of a more homogeneous economic growth on the MSP.

A comparison of five countries with the highest monetary multipliers and five countries with the lowest monetary multipliers[3] is similar to other developing economies in that the lower size of monetary multipliers reflects a lower ratio k and a greater ratio p, while the reverse is true in countries with the highest multipliers.

As in other developing economies, the deterioration in balance-of-payments transactions caused the elimination of foreign exchange transactions as a source for the creation of reserve money, generating a transformation into a significant instrument for reserve money withdrawal (40 percent of the total amount of reserve money creation in late 1983). Within domestic instruments of reserve money creation, the main alteration is apparent in the financing by central banks in the creation of reserve money, while the share of credits to monetary and nonmonetary agents experienced a decline. The rise in the dispersion of percent shares of these instruments in the creation of reserve money reflects the varied impact of exogenous influences. However, a decline in the dispersion of the foreign transactions share in the creation/withdrawal of reserve money does indicate the strong and homogeneous influence of these transactions.

Summary of Conclusions

This group of countries includes economies at a much different level of economic development with a per capita GNP of less than $200 to $4,600. This leads to the expectation, according to the hypothesis on the role played by economic development in the MSP, of great differences in the monetary multipliers, their ratios, and the creation of reserve money. Common characteristics of these countries significant to the MSP reflect indirectly the effects of level of economic development. In turn, this makes the MSP in these countries more homogenized than would appear consistent with the differences in economic development levels as revealed in the per capita GNP. All of the countries involved have a low but differentiated and efficient financial structure (financial institutions and instruments) that include greater involvement by monetary institutions in domestic and foreign financing and central bank action in transactions performed by commercial banks in industrial countries. In addition, the relatively weaker position and greater sensitivity of these countries to the foreign markets and any deterioration in them that could be reflected in less successful balance-of-payments transactions and in a greater deficit of current account balance of payments significantly affect the MSP of these countries, unlike industrial countries and developing oil-exporting countries.

During this period, the impact of the economic character on the MSP was a result of (1) an increase in the deficit of current account balance-of-payments from the second increase in oil prices; (2) decrease in export prices of raw materials (export goods of these economies); (3) protective foreign trade measures by industrial countries (the main importers of these goods); (4) increase in foreign debt service ratio, accompanied by a decrease in foreign exchange reserves; (5) unavoidable restrictive monetary policy measures under these conditions; (6) increase in the deficit of central governments, with increased central bank credits imposed by the central government.

1. These economic developments influence the MSP through significantly lower monetary multipliers in these economies than those of industrial countries, as corresponding to the hypothesis on the economic development role of the MSP. However, the empirical evidence does not prove the hypothesis if monetary multipliers of the three subgroups of countries involved are considered. On the contrary, the decreasing order of economic level of these subgroups is accompanied by an increasing order of monetary multipliers that suggests that under the normal conditions of low differentiation and efficiency of the financial structure,

the influence of exogenous causes is more important than the level of economic development.

2. A decrease in monetary multipliers under study appears similar to their development in industrial countries and oil-exporting developing economies. The main reason for this decline in monetary multipliers has been an increase in the leakage of money with a corresponding decrease in ratio k. This evolved from a deterioration in balance-of-payments transactions, imposing increased foreign borrowing, with a corresponding decrease in the foreign exchange reserves of monetary institutions and a withdrawal of money and the transformation of net foreign assets into net foreign liabilities in these institutions. A lower ratio k was accompanied by a relatively lower decrease in leakage and entropy of reserve money (ratio p), which partly compensated for the impact caused by the decrease in ratio k on monetary multipliers.

3. A deterioration in balance-of-payments of these countries contributed to radical changes in reserve money creation by domestic instruments involving increased central bank credits to the central government to finance increased deficits and an increase in extraordinary financial intervention by central banks resulting from a deteriorating economic development climate.

These exogenous influences had a different effect on the MSP in the individual countries at the different economic development levels that contributed to an increase in the dispersion of monetary multipliers, their ratios, and the creation of reserve money.

The increase in income velocity of money in circulation in these economies evolved from the prevailing dominant restrictive monetary policy.

In this way, the three subgroups of non–oil-exporting developing economies at different economic development levels appear bound together by the significant common characteristics of the MSP. These may also be interpreted as a separate group of countries, although wide differences exist in the levels of economic development within these three subgroups of countries and their per capita GNP.

SOCIALIST ECONOMIES WITH DECENTRALIZED ECONOMIC DECISIONMAKING

For an understanding of the empirical evidence on the MSP, the most important characteristics of these economies are (1) the wide differences in the institutional economic systems of the countries themselves, resulting from the differences in the concept of a socialist economy with decentralized economic decisionmaking; (2) differences in ideological background;

and (3) the rapid evolution of these new economic systems in meaningful varieties of institutional change. All of these characteristics contribute to the wide range of differences in the MSP. The structure of monetary and financial organization within this framework is rather specific: It involves central banks and a simplified structure of other financial organizations—mostly specialized and commercial banks, which are government owned and controlled and not profit oriented, even in countries with a more decentralized banking system, e.g., Yugoslavia. This makes their behavior different from private banks in capitalist economies. Logically, this leads to the MSP's greater dependence on the institutional and financial structure, government measures, and reduced level of dependence on economic developments contributing to greater differences in the MSP. With the small number of countries involved, the possibilities for reaching general conclusions are reduced, as these economies are analyzed by levels of economic development. However, the stronger role for the institutional structure of the economic system makes the summary conclusions on the MSP important in these types of economies.

Per Capita GNP $830–$4,600

There are only two countries classified in this group: Syrian Arab Republic and Yugoslavia. Both have a significantly different ideological and institutional character and economic policies reflective of the wide differences between these countries in the MSP. The most outstanding similarity is the same monetary multiplier at the end of 1978. However, this common multiplier experienced a radical change in the period under study, with a decrease for Syria to 0.8 percent and an increase for Yugoslavia to 1.7 percent at the close of 1983. These changes in the basic ratios k and p reflect the different influences of the balance of payments and economic policy measures.

Another shared characteristic in the MSP of these two economies is in the role of foreign exchange transactions in reserve money creation. Beginning with these transactions as a source for reserve money creation in late 1978, deteriorating balance-of-payments transactions contributed to the transformation from a source of creation into an instrument of reserve money withdrawal, especially in Yugoslavia. The trend throughout the entire period showed the main domestic instrument for reserve money creation in Syria to be central bank credits to the central government, while in Yugoslavia the main source for reserve money creation is central bank credits to other monetary institutions in a fiscal policy rule of no central government budget deficit.

Per Capita GNP $360–$829

This group of four socialist economies provides a better basis for conclusions because there exists a greater homogeneity of monetary multipliers and ratios than in the first group, in spite of their wide institutional and economic differences. The explanation focuses on the institutional components and policy measures relevant for the MSP in (1) a nondifferentiated financial structure, (2) broad regulations of financial transactions performed by public-owned and nonprofit financial organizations, (3) broad regulations for foreign exchange transactions, (4) close ties between central bank, central government, and other monetary institutions, (5) major dependence by other monetary institutions on central bank financing, and (6) strong government control over the activities of public enterprise, income distribution, savings, and investments. Within this framework, a wide range of differences exists in the MSP in comparison with the capitalist economies at the same economic development level and even at other levels of economic development.

The increase in monetary multipliers appears rather specific when compared with the general tendency of decreasing monetary multipliers in other groups of economies. The monetary multiplier began relatively high in these economies in late 1978 and, after a significant increase between 1979 and 1983, it attained the same level as in industrial economies at the end of 1983. This increase in monetary multipliers was accomplished despite a decrease in k ratio that resulted from a deteriorating balance-of-payments current account, a rise in decreasing entropy, and leakage of reserve money (p ratio).

The main contribution to the relatively high and increasing dispersion of coefficients comes mainly from ratios related to the Yemen People's Democratic Republic. The dispersion of ratios of the individual economies is far less pronounced if this country is excluded.

Although the structure of reserve money creation did not change, foreign exchange transactions, as instruments for reserve money withdrawal, did accelerate to a higher rate because of deteriorating balance-of-payments transactions. Within the realm of domestic instruments of reserve money creation, central bank credits to the central government remained the major source for reserve money creation. The share of central bank credits to nonmonetary institutions, along with extraordinary central bank intervention in financing, definitely increased, although the share of central bank credits to other monetary institutions remained unchanged.

Per Capita GNP Less than $360

The involvement of only Tanzania and Ethiopia, with their wide differences in monetary multipliers and relevant ratios, undermines the use of their experience in the MSP as a basis for general conclusions. The MSP in these economies is reflected in the stability of their monetary multipliers and relevant ratios from strong government regulations. The main economic influence on the MSP comes from a deterioration in balance-of-payments transactions reflected in the significant decrease in reserve money creation by foreign exchange transactions in one of these economies and transformation of these transactions from a source of creation to an instrument for reserve money withdrawal in the other.

Summary of Conclusions

Eight countries with significant institutional and ideological differences are included in this institutional economic system on three levels of economic development. Empirical evidence about the differentiated structure of a small number of economies does not provide a proper basis for general conclusions. However, it does present opportunities for a better understanding of the MSP within this differentiated group of countries.

Despite the wide range of differences in these economies, they do share (1) a simplified financial institutional structure and financial instruments that are mainly public owned and nonprofit monetary and other financial institutions that are heavily dependent on borrowing from the central bank; (2) a strong influence exerted by the central government on the central bank and other monetary institutions and the entire financial structure; (3) no financial markets; (4) broad regulation of economic development, income distribution, savings, investments, and balance-of-payments transactions. All of these features of the economies involved are reflected in the MSP. The low profile of economic and market transactions in the MSP reflects these common threads, so attention focuses on the institutional structure and economic policy measures of the MSP in these economies.

As a result, this explains the wide differences in monetary multipliers, relevant ratios, and structure of reserve money creation in countries at the same level of economic development. The most homogeneous group appears to be those countries at the medium level of economic development ($360–$829 per capita GNP) that includes the largest number of economies (4), compared with the two economies included in each of the other two groups of countries with this type of economic system.

However, it is difficult to determine whether these differences are the result of a lower homogeneity in the other two groups of countries or the small number of countries involved.

In spite of wide differences, several common characteristics of the MSP emerge: (1) monetary multipliers are significantly higher than in other groups of economies at the same level of economic development; (2) this is the result of the relatively low entropy and leakage of reserve money (p ratio), while the k ratio (leakage of money) is low from the deficit in the balance-of-payments current account.

An increase in monetary multipliers is revealed in the MSP of these economies, although there is a decrease in the monetary multipliers of other economies in this period. This can be attributed to decreased entropy and leakage of reserve money (ratio p), with leakage of money (accelerating decrease in ratio k) contributing to the decline in monetary multipliers.

In order to increase the money supply in these economies, both reserve money and money multipliers were increased. The creation of reserve money in foreign transactions performed as an instrument for reserve money withdrawal from 1979 to late 1983, following a pattern of other developing economies with deteriorating balance of payments during this period. In late 1978, foreign exchange transactions became instruments for the creation of reserve money in some economies. The creation of reserve money through domestic instruments proves to be rather different, primarily reflecting differences in the (1) decentralization of the banking system, and (2) relationships between the central bank and the central government. Then the main source for reserve money creation came through central bank credits to the central government. Increasing participation by central banks in domestic financial transactions continued to be a significant force in reserve money creation.

SOCIALIST ECONOMIES WITH CENTRALIZED ECONOMIC DECISIONMAKING

The three countries involved in this type of economy are those presented in the *International Financial Statistics* of the International Monetary Fund, although key statistical information about these economies is lacking for this analysis. Hungary, Rumania, and China appear in this analysis, making general conclusions on the MSP difficult to reach, although it is possible to analyze differences in the MSP of these types of economic systems. This is particularly significant if these three economies are considered to be representative of three different concepts and accompanying levels of economic reform: (1) Rumania has made no significant reforms; (2) China is engaged in significant economic reforms; and (3) Hungary has made the greatest progress in economic reforms among the three. With the high degree of homogeneity in the basic institutional structure and policy goals in this type of institutional economic system, the involvement of "reformed" economies proves all the more useful for study in this analysis than if only the orthodox varieties of economies were included.

The basic interconnecting threads of these economies show (1) centrally planned and regulated income, savings, and investments, with scant leeway for financial intermediation; (2) full regulation of foreign exchange transactions; and (3) centrally controlled financial institutions—predominantly a monobanking system. Economic reforms in these economies involve some degree of decentralization in decisionmaking by socialist enterprises, especially in income distribution in investment and greater opportunities for private economic activity in agriculture, with no significant changes in monetary and financial organization.

However, the monetary and financial organization remained strongly centralized and centrally controlled, although the statistical information on transactions by monetary institutions presented in the *International Financial Statistics* presents an illusion of significant differences among these economies. The banking performed by the central bank of China is presented as a monobanking system, with all financial transactions, including the transactions of specialized banks for financing agriculture. Transactions by specialized banks in Rumania are presented separately from central bank transactions, which gives an impression of some decentralization in banking operations.

The impression of some decentralization in banking operations in Hungary is strengthened by the exclusion of commercial bank transactions performed by the central bank of Hungary from the central bank balance sheet; these operations are presented as commercial bank operations on a separate balance sheet of the central bank.

In this way, the existing statistical information presents the similar structure and nature of the MSP in these economies in a rather different way. In China, the MSP is a specific process fundamentally different from the MSP in economies with decentralized economic decisionmaking and a decentralized banking system, while in Rumania these differences appear to be far less; however, in Hungary, there are no apparent differences in the MSP structure. Thus, the MSP in Hungary appears closer to the decentralized economies than to the MSP in Rumania and especially in China, although the MSP in all three economies is fundamentally very similar but different by comparison with decentralized economic decisionmaking economies, both capitalist and socialist.

Per Capita GNP Less than $360

China is a country at the lowest level of economic development. The *International Financial Statistics* presents its MSP as a process within the framework of the monobanking system (the Agricultural Bank is represented as part of the central bank).

Within this framework, the monetary multiplier has a specific content and meaning. In view of the negligible impact of foreign exchange transactions on creation and leakage of money and creation of reserve money, it appears that the amount of reserve money created by the central bank ($_cA$) is the amount of total bank credits (A), so the monetary multiplier reflects only the leakage of money into nonmonetary deposits with the central bank ($m = 1 - t$). Therefore, the low monetary multiplier of China (0.6 percent in the whole period under consideration) cannot be compared with the monetary multipliers of other economies involving the interbank multiplication of reserve money created by the central banking system.

The same conclusion may be reached on the specific nature and noncomparability with economies having decentralized banking systems (including the central bank and other monetary institutions) is also valid for the creation of reserve money. Under a monobanking system, the only instruments for domestic creation of reserve money may be central bank credits to the central government, socialist enterprises, and other nonmonetary institutions. Considering central bank credits to the central government in a socialist centralized economy to be insignificant under the full power of the central government in financial regulation and income distribution, the only source for reserve money creation by domestic instruments is central bank credits to nonmonetary units. This rule may be changed significantly by creation/withdrawal of reserve money by foreign exchange transactions. However, statistical evidence shows that the balance-of-payments equilibrium is reflected in the relatively small share of reserve money creation from these transactions in the example of China.

The highly stable ratios in the MSP of China reflect primarily the stability of government regulations and money/finance measures in this period.

Per Capita GNP $830–$4,600

This group of economies with centralized economic decisionmaking includes two economies at opposite ends of economic reform: Rumania at the lowest (zero) and Hungary at the highest level of economic reform. Empirical evidence shows that the basic characteristics of the MSP in these two economies, if differences in statistical presentation are interpreted properly, are similar not only to each other but to the MSP in China as well.

In the economies of Rumania and Hungary, low monetary multipliers can be observed (0.42 percent and 0.83 percent in late 1983). These low multipliers reflect a relatively high leakage of money (low k ratio) from withdrawal of money by foreign exchange transactions because of a significant deficit in the balance-of-payments current account. A striking difference appears in the entropy and leakage of reserve money (p ratio) to reveal a lower monetary multiplier in Rumania than in Hungary. Once again, this difference in the p ratios, which results from larger deposits with the central bank of Rumania than the central bank of Hungary, represents a statistical illusion reflecting a different presentation for the same deposits. For example, in Rumania they are presented as deposits with the central bank, while in Hungary they are presented as deposits with the commercial banks within the central banking system. If uniformly presented, ratio p in these two economies would disappear, leaving a greater difference in ratio k in determining the monetary multiplier in the same way as China ($m = 1 - t$).

The creation of reserve money in both economies is marked by a withdrawal of reserve money through foreign exchange transactions, although this happens to a lesser degree in Rumania because of a lower deficit in the balance-of-payments current account than in Hungary. A common characteristic of the domestic instruments structure in reserve money creation is that central bank credits to the central government are rather low in Hungary or nonexistent in Rumania; this is the logical result of the powerful financial regulations of the central government that eliminated the need for borrowing.

However, these two countries differ in their other sources for reserve money creation. For example, in Hungary it appears that reserve money is almost equally created by central bank credits to commercial banks and nonmonetary units, while in Rumania the main source for reserve money creation is credits to nonmonetary units. Again, this is a reflection of the different statistical presentations by central bank transactions while the real nature of reserve money creation by domestic instruments is similar in both economies—China, too—in credits to socialist enterprises.

Summary of Conclusions

This group includes only three countries with statistical information available from the *International Financial Statistics*. Because of this, most of these types of economies have been excluded from analysis. The similar institutional structure of these economies, especially in monetary and financial organization, provides a basis for the conclusion that they are properly represented in this analysis, which includes economies at the highest and lowest levels of economic development.

Another logical conclusion that similarity in institutional structure in the monetary and financial organization should be reflected in a similar MSP is not supported by statistical evidence because of the different statistical presentation by central bank transactions in these three economies.

As a result, the structure of the MSP in China is presented within the framework of a monobanking system, while in Rumania and Hungary, separate commercial bank transactions are statistically involved. The basic structure and the nature of bank operations in these three economies are very similar; consequently, after interpretation, the logical conclusion is that the MSP in these economies is basically similar, not being empirically disproved.

After this approach, it may be concluded that the common thread running through the MSP in these economies is the specific nature and relatively low monetary multipliers, including only leakage and creation of money, not reserve money, determined more by regulations and policy measures than by autonomous transactions. In this way, no monetary multiplication process can be observed in economies with decentralized economic decisionmaking and decentralized financial institutions. Central bank investment, representing total investments by monetary institutions, is accompanied by the investment structure involving credits to nonmonetary units or socialist enterprises—different in comparison with decentralized economic decisionmaking economies.

Foreign exchange transactions have had little influence on the MSP because of full government control over balance-of-payments transactions. This remains firmly in place in the MSP in these economies.

NOTES

1. This classification, instead of a classification of countries with monetary multipliers below $m - \sigma$ and above $m + \sigma$ (applied in analyzing this question in other groups of countries), is used because there are no countries with a monetary multiplier below $m - \sigma$ in this group.

2. Argentina is excluded here, with a 340-fold increase in money supply.

3. This classification is applied for similar reasons as in industrial countries. Here there is only one country having a monetary multiplier greater than $m + \sigma$.

7

Structural Comparative Analysis of the Money Supply Process: Late 1983

A structural analysis of the MSP is designed to present and explain differences in the MSP in different types of institutional economic systems and different levels of economic development. This structural comparative analysis of the MSP includes three parts:

1. Comparative analysis of the MSP in a static sense to explain differences in the MSP (creation of reserve money structure, monetary multipliers, and relevant ratios) at the end of 1983.

2. Comparative analysis of the MSP in a combined static and dynamic sense that shows the initial static position of the MSP in late 1978, proceeding to the flows of the MSP from 1979 to 1983, leading to the changes apparent in the creation of reserve money, monetary multipliers, and their relevant ratios at the close of 1983.

3. Explanation of the role of the institutional sectors in the MSP that involves the role of the central banking system, other monetary institutions, nonmonetary domestic sectors, and the rest of the world.

COMPARATIVE ANALYSIS OF MSP

According to the basic equation of creation of money, the analysis of the MSP covers two basic topics: comparative analysis of reserve money

Table 7.1
Monetary Multipliers (Late 1983)

	Average monetary multipliers (m)			Vertically the highest m = 1			Horizontally the highest m = 1		
	CE	SDE	SCE	CE	SDE	SCE	CE	SDE	SCE
IE	1.56	–	–	1.00	–	–	1.00	–	–
OILC	0.89	–	–	0.57	–	–	1.00	–	–
DGE	0.95	1.45	0.62	0.61	0.95	0.97	0.66	1.00	0.43
DGEH	0.81	1.27	0.64	0.52	0.84	1.00	0.64	1.00	0.50
DGEM	1.02	1.51	–	0.65	1.00	–	0.67	1.00	–
DGEL	1.02	1.52	0.58	0.65	1.00	0.91	0.67	1.00	0.38

Source: International Financial Statistics (country pages).

```
   CE=capitalist economies
  SDE=socialist economies with decentralized economic
      decisionmaking
  SCE=socialist economies with centralized economic
      decisionmaking
   IE=industrial economies
 OILC=oil-exporting countries
  DGE=developing non-oil-exporting economies
 DGEH=developing non-oil-exporting economies, $830-4,600
      per capita GNP
 DGEM=developing non-oil-exporting economies, $360-829
      per capita GNP
 DGEL=developing non-oil-exporting economies, less than
      $360 per capita GNP
```

creation (cA) and the monetary multiplication of this money as reflected in the monetary multiplier (m).

Comparative Analysis of Monetary Multipliers

Empirical evidence shows that the highest monetary multiplier may be observed in industrial countries at the highest level of economic development (see table 7.1); this is consistent with the hypothesis above. However, the lowest multipliers cannot be observed in countries at the lowest level of economic development. The slightly increasing order of monetary multipliers in developing countries accompanying a decreasing order of economic development level are apparent in both capitalist and socialist economies with decentralized economic decisionmaking.

The behavior of monetary multipliers, particularly the rather low monetary multiplier in developing oil-exporting countries with the highest per capita GNP—higher than that of industrial economies—may appear contradictory to the hypothesis on the role that the level of economic development plays in the monetary multiplication process. As explained in a holistic analysis of the MSP, the behavior of monetary multipliers in developing economies does not contradict this hypothesis. In fact, it gives a better insight into the actual role of the level of economic development in the monetary multiplication process. It supports the conclusion that the level of economic development influences monetary multiplication processes primarily through its interrelationship with the degree of differentiation and efficiency of the financial organization.

Thus, the main relevant difference between industrial economies and developing economies appears to be the difference in the degree of differentiation and efficiency of financial organization in financial institutions, financial markets, and financial instruments. This difference is small within developing economies, regardless of the differences in per capita GNP, the symbol of the level of economic development in these countries. Therefore, a more significant contribution may be the exogenous or random influences contributing to the contradictory behavior of the monetary multipliers of developing economies under these conditions.

Considering the monetary multipliers of the different economic systems, it appears that monetary multipliers are at the highest level in socialist economies with decentralized economic decisionmaking (SDE)—similar to monetary multipliers in industrial economies, although at a far lower level of economic development and less differentiated financial organization. This proves the hypothesis that the institutional structure of the economic system has a very significant influence on the monetary multiplication process, as empirical evidence will reveal. The same is more valid for the lower monetary multipliers in socialist economies with centralized economic decisionmaking (SCE) than in other economic systems, particularly compared with monetary multipliers in SDE.

According to the explanations already presented, the monetary multiplier is determined by the leakage of money (ratio k) and the entropy and leakage of reserve money (ratio p), i.e., $m = k:p$. The arithmetic means of these two basic ratios determining the size of monetary multipliers—similar in a holistic analysis—are used to explain differences in average monetary multipliers of the above groups of countries.[1]

Table 7.2
Leakage and Entropy of Reserve Money (p) and Money Supply (k): Arithmetic Means (Late 1983)

	Leakage of Money Supply (k)			Leakage and Entropy of Reserve Money (p)		
	CE	SDE	SCE	CE	SDE	SCE
IE	0.27	–	–	0.20	–	–
OILC	0.65	–	–	1.60	–	–
DGE	0.37	0.43	0.39	0.43	0.38	0.69
DGEH	0.29	0.33	0.27	0.42	0.34	0.50
DGEM	0.37	0.42	–	0.41	0.36	–
DGEL	0.46	0.54	0.62	0.48	0.44	1.07

Source: International Financial Statistics (country pages).

The empirical evidence shows that the main determinant in the relationships of the size of monetary multipliers of individual groups of countries in the matrix is the leakage and entropy of reserve money (ratio p)(see table 7.2). Thus, the largest monetary multipliers within capitalist countries (industrial economies) result from relatively low entropy and leakage of reserve money (ratio p) compared with this ratio in developing economies within this economic system. In addition, the relatively low size of p ratio in socialist decentralized economies (SDE) explains the rather low monetary multipliers of these countries. However, the size of p ratio does not explain the slightly increasing order of monetary multipliers of developing economies accompanying the decreasing order of the level of economic development. The ratio k offers an explanation for this phenomenon.

Empirical evidence shows that the leakage of money (ratio k) mainly has different effects on the size of monetary multipliers by groups of economies when compared with those of leakage and entropy of reserve money (ratio p). In the case of industrial economies, the rather low ratio k significantly compensates for the effects of a very low ratio p. The opposite effect is observable in oil-exporting economies where a high ratio k reduces the effect of a very high ratio p on the monetary multipliers of these economies. Significant effects of ratio k are observed in capitalist economies and socialist economies at the same level of economic development. In capitalist developing economies, the lower ratio k strengthens the effect of a relatively higher ratio p, while in socialist decentralized economies, a relatively larger ratio k produces a stronger environment for the relatively low ratio p of the monetary multiplier in these economies. The relatively low ratio k in socialist centralized economies contributes to a lower monetary multiplier, while being parallel with the relatively high ratio p in these economies, making the monetary multiplier in these economies the lowest.

A more homogeneous effect of leakage of money (ratio k) is found in the level of economic development. For example, ratio k follows the rule of higher k at a lower level of economic development, which contributes to the apparent paradox that the hypothesis of a higher monetary multiplier at a higher level of economic development is empirically justified in comparing industrial and developing economies but not in monetary multipliers within the three subgroups of developing economies. This hypothesis appears valid in developing economies in leakage and entropy of reserve money (ratio p increasing parallel with decreasing level of economic development). The opposite and stronger effect is obvious in the increasing order of ratio k following the decreasing order of the level of economic development. In this way, the apparent contradictory empirical evidence on the behavior of the monetary multiplier within the three groups of developing economies can be explained through the behavior of ratio k.

The following presentation on the behavior of ratio k will explain this apparent contradiction in the activity of monetary multipliers within developing economies.

Low entropy and leakage of reserve money (p) in industrial countries reflects the higher degree of differentiation and efficiency of financial organization in these economies compared with developing capitalist economies. This is revealed in the low entropy of reserve money (e), in low holding of currency in nonmonetary units (c), and small deposits with the central banking system ($d + ct$). All of these ratios are significantly larger in developing economies (see table 7.3). A lower p ratio in socialist decentralized countries in comparison with capitalist economies at the same level of economic development reflects lower leakage of reserve money in deposits with central banks ($d + ct$) and entropy ratio (e), while the holding of currency by nonmonetary units (c) is greater in these economies. A high p ratio in SCE is a logical result of a relatively

Table 7.3
Entropy and Leakage of Reserve Money Ratios: $p = e + c + d + ct$,
Arithmetic Means (Late 1983)

	Entropy Ratios (e)			Currency in Circulation (c)			Other Central Bank Liabilities $(d + {}_c t)$		
	CE	SDE	SCE	CE	SDE	SCE	CE	SDE	SCE
IE	0.04	–	–	0.08	–	–	0.09	–	–
OILC	0.13	–	–	0.25	–	–	1.21	–	–
DGE	0.09	0.10	0.13	0.20	0.23	0.12	0.15	0.04	0.44
DGEH	0.12	0.09	0.20	0.13	0.17	0.11	0.17	0.08	0.19
DGEM	0.09	0.12	–	0.20	0.23	–	0.13	0.00	–
DGEL	0.07	0.08	–	0.26	0.27	0.15	0.15	0.09	0.92

Source: International Financial Statistics (country pages).

large holding of deposits by nonmonetary units with the central banks $(d + ct)$. In this way, the size of entropy and leakage of reserve money ratio (p) of individual groups of countries may be considered consistent with the logical hypothesis on behavior of economic units under different institutional circumstances and at different levels of economic development. This explains the main reasons for the consistency in the size of monetary multipliers by different groups of countries.

The rather divergent behavior of leakage of money supply (k ratio) reflects the different nature and behavior of its component basic ratios: t ratio presenting leakage of money to nonmonetary deposits with monetary institutions, and f ratio representing leakage or creation of money by foreign exchange transactions by monetary institutions $(k = 1 - t + f)$. The leakage of money into nonmonetary deposits (t) is greatest at the highest level of economic development (industrial countries), reflecting a rather differentiated structure that produces the stimulus for investment of money into nonmonetary deposits and the policy of economic units to invest extra money into these deposits, including a lower demand for money in the narrow sense, if a broad structure of other liquid financial investments is possible. For the same reasons, t ratio is lower (1) in countries at a lower level of economic development, (2) in socialist countries with a lower level of economic development, and (3) in socialist countries with a simplified financial structure based on institutional and ideological reasons. This explains the lower k ratio in industrial countries and higher k ratio in socialist countries, along with capitalist countries at a lower level of economic development.

On the other hand, the size of f ratio reflects both the level of economic development and extraordinary exogenous influences. The level of economic development influences the f ratio through the negative current account of the balance-of-payments transactions and greater involvement of the monetary institutions in foreign transactions. This is why the f ratio is positive in industrial countries (creation of money), even in current account deficits. However, the f ratio is negative (withdrawal of money) in developing economies (excluding oil-exporting economies) with deficits in current accounts of their balance of payments. Deterioration both in the foreign markets and in deficits of current accounts of balance of payments in developing economies were widespread. All economies, except industrial and oil-exporting countries, had a deficit in current accounts balance-of-payments transactions that strongly influenced the net foreign assets position of monetary institutions, as reflected in their negative f ratios at the end of 1983.[2] These developments were reflected in the low foreign financial assets and high foreign liabilities of the monetary institutions of these countries at the end of 1983 (table 7.4).

Empirical evidence on the basic ratios determining monetary multipliers proves the consistency of the size of monetary multipliers by individual groups of economies with the logical hypothesis reflecting the consistency of basic ratios p and k (determining monetary multipliers) with the hypothesis on the influence of the institutional economic system and the level of economic development on these ratios. Some differences between the empirical evidence and the hypothesis can be explained mainly as the result of institutional differences and differences in the level of economic development within the same group of countries that are classified by institutional economic systems, level of economic development, and extraordinary exogenous influences, especially those related to marked deterioration in balance-of-payments transactions in developing economies during this period. Oil-exporting developing economies logically represent that group of countries experiencing the greatest deviations from assumptions about the level of economic development.

Table 7.4
Leakage of Money Supply: Arithmetic Means of Ratios (Late 1983)

	Leakage to Nonmonetary Deposits (t)			Effects of Foreign Exchange Transactions (f)			Total Net: f - t		
	CE	SDE	SCE	CE	SDE	SCE	CE	SDE	SCE
IE	1.79	–	–	0.06	–	–	-0.73	–	–
OILC	1.97	–	–	1.62	–	–	-0.35	–	–
DGE	0.54	0.40	0.44	-0.09	-0.18	-0.12	-0.63	-0.58	-0.56
DGEH	0.64	0.49	0.43	-0.08	-0.18	-0.30	-0.72	-0.67	-0.73
DGEM	0.54	0.32	–	-0.10	-0.26	–	-0.64	-0.58	–
DGEL	0.44	0.45	0.45	-0.10	-0.01	-0.07	-0.54	0.46	-0.38

Source: International Financial Statistics (country pages).

Comparative Analysis of Creation of Reserve Money (Late 1983)

Empirical evidence shows sharp differences in the basic structure of reserve money creation between developed and developing economies. In industrial economies, reserve money was created partly by domestic ($_cA_d$) and foreign exchange transactions ($_cE_n$), with both claiming a similar share in total reserve money creation. In developing economies and all economic systems of these economies, foreign exchange transactions represent the instrument for reserve money withdrawal, so that creation of reserve money has been made only by domestic transactions. The logical exception to this rule is the oil-exporting developing economies, and one developing socialist centralized economy, China, at the lowest level of economic development, and with strong control of foreign exchange transactions. Deteriorating balance-of-payments transactions, under conditions of greater involvement by monetary institutions in these transactions, heralded the withdrawal of reserve money by foreign exchange transactions in developing economies. In industrial economies, with more differentiated monetary and financial organization and less sensitivity to balance-of-payments transactions or greater share of non-

Table 7.5
Structure of Reserve Money Creation by Domestic Instruments (Late 1983)

	Claims on Central Government $(_cA_g)$			Claims on Other Monetary $(_cA_m)$			Other Instruments $(_cA_n + _cU_a)$		
	CE	SDE	SCE	CE	SDE	SCE	CE	SDE	SCE
IE	0.38	–	–	0.12	–	–	0.05	–	–
OILC	0.21	–	–	0.11	–	–	0.05	–	–
DGE	0.76	1.17	0.07	0.27	0.29	0.36	0.33	0.37	0.81
DGEH	0.61	0.60	0.08	0.27	0.73	0.71	0.38	0.24	0.72
DGEM	0.82	2.06	–	0.27	0.13	–	0.31	0.65	–
DGEL	0.85	0.84	0.05	0.28	0.02	0.00	0.28	0.21	0.89

Source: International Financial Statistics (country pages).

monetary units in financing these transactions, the impact was less pronounced.

The structure of reserve money creation by domestic instruments was significantly influenced by institutional economic systems and the level of economic level. As a result, a significant differentiation in the structure of reserve money creation by these instruments is apparent (see table 7.5).

In economies with decentralized economic decisionmaking, socialist and capitalist, regardless of the economic development level, the main source for reserve money creation was the financing of the central government by the central banking system in granting credits and buying government securities. The share of central government financing in reserve money creation in socialist centralized economies was not significant. The role of financial intermediation is rather narrow, and the power of the central government in financial matters is very extensive, so that the central government has no need to use central bank or other bank credits for financing.

Central bank claims on other monetary institutions appear to be the second most important source for reserve money creation in capitalist economies at all levels of economic development, but not in socialist economies where financing of nonmonetary units is the second most important source for reserve money creation. This is reflective of (1) the reduced involvement of central banks in capitalist economies in financing of nonmonetary entities, and (2) greater differentiation in the role of other monetary institutions in financing these entities than in socialist economies experiencing greater involvement by central banks, especially in socialist economies with centralized economic decisionmaking in financing socialist enterprises.

The level of economic development appears to generate the large share of extraordinary central bank financing of other net assets in central bank balance sheets to reflect the need for extraordinary central bank intervention in a climate of deteriorating balance-of-payments transactions and worsening domestic economic developments.

Thus, empirical evidence proves the logical hypothesis about the role of institutional economic systems, economic development level, and exogenous influences in the creation of reserve money.

NOTES

1. This equation is fully correct for calculation of monetary multipliers in the individual countries, but it may happen that the calculation of a monetary multiplier for a group of economies by using this formula (application of the arithmetic means of ratios k and p) produces a result different from the size of the average monetary multiplier calculated as an arithmetic mean for monetary multipliers of economies involved. This is a result of different dispersion of monetary multipliers, ratios k, and ratios p within the group of economies. Studies reveal that in spite of these differences in multipliers calculated as an arithmetic mean of multipliers of economies involved in a group, and multipliers calculated by average ratios k and p of these economies, the interrelationships of monetary multipliers of individual groups of economies in the matrix classification of economies are not changed. Thus, it proves that the average ratios k and p can be used to explain these interrelationships—the target for a comparative analysis of monetary multipliers.

2. The exception is China, the only representative of centralized socialist countries at the lowest level of economic development, because of strong balance-of-payments regulations.

8

Structural Comparative Analysis of the Money Supply Process: Late 1978 and 1979–83

A comparative analysis of the MSP focuses on (1) an explanation of the static comparative analysis of the MSP at the end of 1983, resulting from initial static properties of the MSP at the end of 1978, and (2) the dynamic properties of the MSP from 1979 to 1983. For this purpose, the MSP at the end of 1978 is analyzed first to emphasize its differences from the MSP at the end of 1983. The analysis of the MSP (1979–83) then explains the flows involved in the MSP, using the dynamic approach to this analysis, and indicates the influence of these flows on the differences. Within this framework, an analysis of the MSP in 1979–83 includes in its dynamic approach two groups of economic developments observed in this period and their impact on the MSP: (1) the relevant economic changes in economies involved in economic development, and (2) exogenous influences on the MSP through developments, national and international, after the second increase in oil prices.

COMPARATIVE ANALYSIS OF THE MSP: LATE 1978

Monetary multipliers are analyzed first and then the structure of reserve money creation. Empirical evidence suggests the same conclusions on differences in monetary multipliers by institutional economic systems and levels of economic development at the end of 1978 and at the end of 1983. However, a significant characteristic is the higher level of monetary multipliers at the end of 1978 than at the end of 1983, which suggests that monetary multipliers at the end of 1983 reflect a decrease in these multipliers.

In addition, differences in the size of monetary multipliers by institutional economic systems and economic development levels were similarly determined at the end of 1983, primarily by differences in entropy and leakage of reserve money (ratio p). Leakage of money (ratio k) appears to be a significant determinant of the low monetary multipliers only in socialist centralized countries, when combined with their relatively high ratio p. However, these ratios have a specific meaning in these economies. Similar to findings on the MSP at the end of 1983, we may conclude that the size of monetary multipliers by groups of economies and the influence of k and p ratios determining their size are consistent with the logical hypothesis on the role of institutional economic systems and economic development levels in the MSP, and the possible role of exogenous influences on the MSP.

The lowest leakage and entropy of reserve money in industrial economies (ratio p) reflects the lowest of all three components of ratio p: (1) the lowest holding of reserve money by monetary institutions with the central banks (ratio e); (2) the lowest holding of currency by nonmonetary units (ratio c); and (3) the lowest monetary and nonmonetary deposits with the central banks (ratios d and $_cd$). All of these ratios reflect logical behavior within highly differentiated and efficient monetary and financial organization in industrial countries.

Significantly greater leakage and entropy of reserve money in capitalist non–oil-exporting developing economies represent a greater concentration of all three components of ratio p in a climate of less developed financial and monetary organization in these countries. This occurs through greater holding of reserve money by monetary institutions with the central bank through a nonefficient money market; (2) greater holding of currency by nonmonetary units (ratio c); and (3) greater monetary and nonmonetary deposits with the central bank imposed by less differentiated monetary and financial organization.

Entropy and leakage of reserve money (ratio p) are the greatest in oil-exporting developing economies, and are the result of (1) large holdings of reserve money by monetary institutions with the central bank; (2) large holdings of currency by nonmonetary units; and (3) large monetary and nonmonetary deposits of nonmonetary units with central banks.

Entropy and leakage of reserve money (p) in socialist decentralized economies are lower than in capitalist economies at the same level of economic development because of lower holdings of reserve money by monetary institutions with the central bank as a result of (1) the simplified structure of monetary institutions and (2) lower amounts of monetary and nonmonetary deposits of nonmonetary units with central banks ($d + ct$ ratios). Holding currency by nonmonetary units is similar in capitalist economies at the same level of economic development.

A greater p ratio in socialist centralized economies primarily reflects greater holdings of monetary and nonmonetary deposits by nonmonetary units with the central banks under the monetary and financial organization of these economies.

In this way, it may be concluded that the entropy and leakage of reserve money (ratio p), representing the main determinant of differences in monetary multipliers by groups of economies, mainly reflects the influence of the institutional systems and the level of economic development of countries involved. This is consistent with the logical hypothesis of their influence on the MSP in contributing to a better understanding of the root causes of the consistent size of monetary multipliers by country groups and the impact of institutional economic systems and level of economic development.

Lower ratio k in industrial economies results from a high leakage of money into nonmonetary deposits, a reflection of the importance of monetary institutions in stimulating these deposits. Relatively low creation of money by foreign exchange transactions also contributes to a low k ratio despite the relatively better balance-of-payments position of these economies, which reflects the transactions process through low involvement of the monetary institutions and greater participation by nonmonetary units.

A significantly greater k ratio in capitalist non–oil-exporting developing economies is generated by lower nonmonetary deposits with monetary institutions because of a lower savings ratio by households in these deposits and other financial investments. In addition, greater ratio k in these economies reflects a lower withdrawal of money in foreign exchange transactions because of less participation by monetary institutions in foreign borrowing than in holding foreign assets (greater share of importers in foreign borrowing). This reflects a positive ratio f in comparison with the negative ratio f at the end of 1983.

The unusually high k ratio of oil-exporting developing economies evolved from opposite influences of a very high leakage of money into nonmonetary deposits of monetary institutions (t) and a rise in the creation of money by foreign exchange transactions by these institutions, arising logically in economies with high surpluses of balance-of-payments current accounts and less differentiated monetary and financial organizations. In view of the wide range of differences among these economies, the k ratios and the determinant ratios t and f in some countries in this group significantly deviate from the above conclusions and average ratios.

Ratio k in socialist decentralized economies is similar to this ratio in capitalist economies at the same level of economic development and evolved from lower leakage of money into nonmonetary deposits with monetary institutions (t) because of (1) less differentiation and less efficient monetary and financial organization, (2) lower savings ratio by households, (3) leakage of money through foreign exchange transactions by monetary institutions, and (4) greater involvement in financing deficits in current balance-of-payments accounts.

The lowest ratio k in socialist centralized economies reflects a similar leakage of money in nonmonetary deposits with monetary institutions, and is accompanied by greater leakage of money by foreign exchange transactions because of greater involvement by monetary institutions in foreign borrowing and reduced holdings of foreign assets.

The underlying reasons for the differences in ratios k among capitalist economies, socialist economies with decentralized economic decisionmaking, and socialist economies with centralized economic decisionmaking appear to be differences in the leakage of money in nonmonetary deposits and the share of monetary institutions in (1) foreign transactions, (2) foreign borrowing, and (3) holding of foreign exchange and other foreign assets.

As foreign exchange transactions exert an influence on creation/leakage of money supply, there also exists a flow of influence on creation/withdrawal of reserve money transactions. In capitalist economies, both industrial and developing, reserve money is created by domestic and foreign transactions. However, in socialist economies, this money is created predominantly through domestic transactions and the instrument of foreign exchange to execute the withdrawal of reserve money. Within capitalist economies, the greatest share of foreign exchange transactions in reserve money creation is observed in industrial economies and oil-exporting developing economies reflective of their stronger balance-of-payments position than in other capitalist economies as accompanied by greater buying than selling of foreign exchange by the central banking system.

The structure of reserve money creation by domestic instruments in the groups of economies appears primarily influenced by the institutional structure. In countries with decentralized economic decisionmaking, capitalist and socialist, the main instruments for reserve money creation also function as instruments to finance the central government by the central banks/credits and purchase of government securities. The second most important instrument for the creation of reserve money is through central bank financing of other monetary institutions. The least important instrument is central bank crediting of nonmonetary units, reflecting the rule that financing of these units is made mainly by other monetary or nonmonetary financial institutions.

In socialist economies with centralized economic decisionmaking, the structure of reserve money creation is logically different. The main source for reserve money creation appears to be in the crediting of nonmonetary units by central banks. However, a significant share of reserve money creation by crediting of other monetary institutions is apparent, which is mainly a reflection of the commercial banking operations of the central bank in Hungary as transactions of commercial banks. The logical conclusion is that reserve money creation in these economies, along with total bank credits, is generated by granting credits to nonmonetary units or mainly socialist enterprises.

Creation of money at the end of 1978, although significant in comparison with the radical changes in the next periods, is negligible in central bank financing.

CHANGES IN THE MSP: LATE 1978 TO LATE 1983

The explanation of monetary multipliers, their relevant ratios, holistic analysis, and the reserve money creation structure at the end of 1978 and 1983 reveals the following significant changes:

1. The relative size of the average monetary multipliers of groups of countries classified by institutional economic system and level of economic development appears basically unchanged. Some changes in the average size of monetary multipliers in these groups emerge from (1) different changes in monetary multipliers of these groups of economies, (2) decrease in monetary multipliers of capitalist economies and socialist economies with centralized economic decisionmaking, and (3) their increase in socialist economies with decentralized economic decisionmaking.

2. Basically, changes in average monetary multipliers reflect a decrease in k ratios because of an increase in leakage of money supply in all groups of economies except socialist centralized economies, and lower decrease or no change at all in the p ratio and the k ratio in socialist centralized economies. As a result, we see:

— Decrease in monetary multipliers in industrial economies (14 percent) was the result of a decrease in ratio k (21 percent) from late 1983 to late 1978, while ratio p remained unchanged.

— Slight decrease in the monetary multiplier of developing capitalist non–oil-exporting economies (10 percent) was the result of a greater average decrease in ratio k than in ratio p (34 and 30 percent).

— Slight decrease in the monetary multiplier of developing oil-exporting countries (5 percent) reflects a greater decrease in average ratio k than in ratio p (24 and 22 percent).

— Increase in the monetary multiplier of socialist decentralized economies (13 percent) cannot be explained as a reflection of changes in the average ratios k and p (decrease of 20 and 17 percent) because of wide asymmetric dispersion of these ratios by individual economies involved in this group.

— Decrease in the monetary multiplier of socialist centralized economies reflects a greater increase in ratio p (21 percent) than in ratio k (11 percent).

3. Decrease in ratio p, except in industrial capitalist and socialist centralized economies, results from a decreased supply and increased demand in financial markets, restrictive monetary policy measures, and government measures designed to improve the balance of payments by decreasing domestic demand for goods. All of these factors influence lower entropy and leakage of reserve money. In developing economies, lower entropy, leakage of reserve money, and decrease in ratio p were the result of escalating differentiation and more efficient financial organization in the economic development process.

— In industrial countries, the unchanged ratio p is caused by the opposite effects of changes in entropy and leakage of reserve money. On one hand, a 27 percent decrease in entropy of reserve money (e) and a 23 percent decrease in currency held in circulation (c) have contributed to a decrease in ratio p. On the other hand, an 88 percent increase in nonmonetary deposits held with the central banking systems from restrictive monetary policy measures and balance-of-payments regulations has compensated for the impact of lower entropy and leakage of reserve money into currency in circulation. As a result, the total amount of entropy and leakage of reserve money have remained relatively unchanged (ratio p).

— In developing capitalist economies, oil-exporting, and non–oil-exporting economies, a decrease in ratio p reflects a decrease in all components of entropy and leakage of reserve money (e,c,ct).

— In socialist economies with decentralized economic decisionmaking, a decrease in ratio p of 17 percent was the result of a 21 percent decrease in reserve money leakage into currency in circulation (ratio c) and a 60 percent decrease in leakage of reserve money into nonmonetary deposits with the central banks. However, a 45 percent increase in entropy of reserve money (e) reflects less sensitivity by monetary institutions in these economies to economic criteria that compensates for the effects of lower leakage of reserve money (c,ct).

— Increased ratio p in socialist economies with centralized economic decisionmaking reflects a 44 percent increase in entropy of reserve money (e), a 20 percent increase in leakage of reserve money in currency in circulation (c), and a 16 percent increase in deposits with the central banking system (d, ct). However, both entropy and leakage of reserve money in these economies reflect the idiosyncrasies of government and central bank regulations.

4. A decrease in k ratio reflects an increased leakage of the money supply as the result of an increase in leakage of money through foreign exchange transactions by monetary institutions and reduction in the creation of money through these transactions (f) from (1) a deterioration in balance of payments, (2) increase in controlling foreign exchange regulation, and (3) increased dependence on financing balance-of-payments transactions by monetary institutions in developing economies. This interaction evokes this sequence of events:

— Decreased ratio k in industrial economies (21 percent) was the result of 40 percent lower creation of money by foreign exchange transaction (f = 0.10 in 1978; 0.06 in 1983), which was accompanied by a 4 percent increase in leakage of money into nonmonetary deposits (t = 0.79 in 1983, 0.76 in 1978).

— In developing non–oil-exporting capitalist economies, a 34 percent decrease in ratio k was exclusively the result of a transformation in foreign exchange transactions from a source for creation of money into an instrument for leakage of money (f = 0.19 in 1978 and −0.09 in 1983). At the same time, leakage of money into nonmonetary deposits experienced a 14 percent decrease because of a restrictive monetary policy and lower savings ratio by households because of a lower rate of increase or decrease in the GNP; this partly compensated for the impact of foreign exchange transactions by monetary institutions.

— Similar causes contributed to a decrease in ratio k in developing oil-exporting countries (24 percent). Creation of money by foreign exchange transactions was lower (f = 1.87 in 1978 and 1.62 in 1983), accompanied by 2 percent lower leakage of money into nonmonetary deposits with monetary institutions (t = 2.01 in 1978 and 1.97 in 1983).

— In decentralized socialist economies, a 17 percent decrease in ratio k reflects an increase in the withdrawal of money in foreign exchange transactions by monetary institutions (f = −0.01 in 1978 and −0.18 in 1983) from deteriorating balance of payments; this partly compensated for the decrease in the leakage of money into nonmonetary deposits with monetary institutions by 11 percent (t = 0.45 in 1978 and 0.40 in 1983) from causes similar to those in developing capitalist countries.

— A contrasting development of ratio k in socialist centralized economies (11 percent increase) mainly reflects the effects of government regulations on relevant transactions leading to a 33 percent decrease in leakage of money through foreign exchange transactions (f = −0.18 in 1978 and −0.12 in 1983), accompanied by a slightly lower leakage of money into nonmonetary deposits with monetary institutions (t = 0.46 in 1978 and 0.44 in 1983).

5. The structure of reserve money creation was significantly changed by deteriorating balance-of-payments accounts in developing economies where monetary institutions are strongly involved in foreign financial transactions that reflect increased government regulations and central bank interventions.

— The greatest changes are observed in the role of foreign exchange transactions in reserve money creation in developing, non–oil-exporting economies. There foreign exchange transactions represented instruments for reserve money creation in late 1978 (16 percent of the total cA), and in late 1983 these transactions appear as instruments for reserve money withdrawal (35 percent of total cA). Similar direction in change in the creation of reserve money structure can be observed in socialist decentralized economies, where these transactions represented instruments for withdrawal of reserve money amounting to 10 percent of total cA at the end of 1978, while this percentage of withdrawal of reserve money was increased to 83 percent at the end of 1983. In socialist centralized economies, the government and central bank regulations evolved from (1) a lower share of withdrawal of reserve money by foreign exchange transactions, and (2) withdrawal of reserve money amounting to 29 percent of cA at the end of 1978 and 22 percent at the end of 1983. In industrial economies, no change in the role of foreign exchange transactions as instruments for reserve money creation is detected (46 percent of total cA at the end of both 1978 and 1983 reflect low dependence of monetary institutions on changes in balance-of-payments accounts). In oil-exporting developing economies, an increase in the share of foreign exchange transactions in reserve money creation was 58 percent at the end of 1978 and 63 percent at the end of 1983) as a result of improved balance-of-payments accounts and the strong influence of these accounts on the net foreign assets position of monetary institutions.

— The above changes in the share of foreign exchange transactions of monetary institutions in reserve money creation (cA) meant at the same time opposite changes in reserve money creation by domestic transactions by central banks that imposed appropriate changes in the instrument structure of domestic creation of reserve money. In groups of economies with larger changes in the share of reserve money creation by foreign exchange/domestic instruments, broader changes occurred in the domestic instruments structure for the creation of reserve money. First, there was no significant change in the domestic instrument structure for creation of reserve money in industrial economies, oil-exporting developing economies, and socialist economies with centralized economic decisionmaking. Significant changes in the instrument structure were prominent in non–oil-developing capitalist economies and socialist economies with decentralized economic decisionmaking. Second, the share of domestic instruments in reserve money creation in non–oil-exporting developing capitalist economies increased through (a) increasing the share of central government financing by central banks (48 percent of total $_cA$ at the end of 1978 and 76 percent at the end of 1983); and (b) effecting significant extraordinary financial transactions by central banks ($_cU_a$) under deteriorating conditions in balance-of-payments accounts and domestic economic developments (2 percent in 1978; 19 percent in 1983). The share of reserve money creation by regular financing of nonmonetary units and monetary institutions ($_cA_n$ and $_cA_m$) experienced a slight increase in their share in creation of reserve money. Third, in socialist economies with decentralized economic decisionmaking, the increase in withdrawal of reserve money by foreign exchange transactions was covered by (a) an increase in the share of central government financing by central banks (81 percent of the total $_cA$ at the end of 1978 and 117 percent at the end of 1983), and (b) extraordinary financial transactions by central banks (17 percent of $_cA$ at the end of 1983, with negligible transactions at the end of 1978). In these economies the increase in the share of central bank credits to nonmonetary units was also significant (10 percent of $_cA$ at the end of 1978, 20 percent at the end of 1983).

DYNAMIC COMPARATIVE ANALYSIS OF THE MSP: 1979–83

This comparative analysis of the MSP is based on a dynamic approach designed to explain changes in stock monetary multipliers, their ratios, and the creation of reserve money at the end of 1983, compared with those at the beginning of 1978. As previously discussed, the analysis of flow monetary multipliers is to interpret these multipliers—interrelated with stock monetary multipliers and creation of reserve money structure—in their role as part of the whole analysis of the MSP. Both stock and flow (static and dynamic) analysis of the MSP are based on (1) wealth approach theories of the behavior of the economic units that are motivated by optimal portfolio selection goals; (2) flow ratio analyses that include the current causes of changes in the MSP; and (3) changes in domestic and foreign economic developments, including economic and monetary policy measures.

Significant differences have evolved from stock and flow ratios that include greater increases or decreases in flow ratios than increases or decreases in stock ratios, evoking greater changes in stock ratios if the differences are greater.

In this way, a dynamic analysis of the MSP represents that part of the analysis of the MSP that involves investigation of (1) the same motives of behavior, (2) economic policy measures, and (3) economic environment as a static analysis of the MSP. Wide differences in monetary multipliers, relevant ratios, and creation of reserve money structure are revealed when compared with those in a static analysis where monetary multipliers are analyzed before the creation of reserve money structure.

The reduced flow monetary multipliers (1979–83) at the end of 1978 explain the decrease in stock multipliers in late 1983 in industrial countries, non–oil-exporting developing countries, and socialist centralized countries. In contrast, the greater flow monetary multiplier (1979–83) explains the increase in the stock monetary multiplier in decentralized socialist countries. However, the increased flow monetary multipliers (1979–83) do not explain the lower stock multiplier (late 1983 compared with late 1978) in oil-exporting developing countries. This contradictory development of stock and flow multipliers during this period is the result of the effects of a very high dispersion of monetary multipliers in these countries, as reflected in the distorted average size of stock and flow multipliers of these countries.

The relative size of flow monetary multipliers by economic systems and levels of economic development appears similar to stock multipliers, including the contradictory but increasing order of monetary multipliers accompanying the decreasing order of economic development of non-oil-exporting developing capitalist countries. However, a significant exception is present in the flow monetary multipliers of socialist decentralized economies with higher flow monetary multipliers than those of industrial countries. The other exception within these countries is that the decreasing order of economic development level is not followed by an increasing order of monetary multipliers observed in stock multipliers at the end of 1978.

Similar to stock monetary multipliers, the differences in the size of flow monetary multipliers by economic systems are mainly determined by ratio p, indicating the degree of entropy and leakage of reserve money. In addition, differences in these multipliers because of economic development levels were significantly influenced by ratio k, indicating leakage of money supply. In this respect, flow monetary multipliers follow the rule of stock multipliers that greater ratio k is observed at a lower level of economic development, but the relatively greater ratio p overcompensates for the impact of a greater ratio k; consequently, the monetary multipliers in industrial countries are significantly greater than multipliers in developing countries. Evidence that this rule does not apply in developing capitalist countries is apparent in flow monetary multipliers.

The role of ratio k in the differences of flow monetary multipliers compared with stock multipliers appears more significant than that of ratio p. In industrial economies, a lower flow multiplier reflects a decrease in ratio k (0.19, compared with 0.34 at the end of 1978), while ratio p remained nearly unchanged. A decrease in the flow monetary multiplier in non–oil-exporting developing capitalist economies reflects a stronger decrease in ratio k (39 percent) than the decrease in ratio p (30 percent) compared with these ratios at the end of 1978. Similar effects of ratios k and p are observed in developing oil-exporting countries experiencing a decrease in the monetary multiplier of 6 percent with a greater decrease in ratio k (33 percent) than in ratio p (31 percent). In socialist decentralized economies, the higher average monetary multiplier (69 percent) cannot be explained by changes in average ratios k and p (decrease in ratio k of 31 percent and in ratio p of 29 percent), which indicates a decrease, not increase, in monetary multiplier because of wide asymmetric dispersion of these ratios. In socialist centralized economies, a flow monetary multiplier 34 percent lower than at the end of 1978 reflects a greater increase in ratio p (68 percent) than in ratio k (31 percent).

Similar to an analysis of the determinants of stock monetary multipliers, closer analysis of determinants of ratios k and p in flow monetary multipliers mainly proves the hypothesis on the role of the institutional economic system and level of economic development in the MSP, which indicates the significant role of exogenous influences on the MSP in the decrease of flow monetary multipliers in nearly all groups of these countries.

The low entropy and leakage of reserve money (ratio p) in industrial economies is consistent with the relatively low entropy of reserve money (ratio e): (1) low demand for reserve money by monetary institutions; (2) low demand for currency reflected in the low leakage of reserve money into currency in circulation (ratio c); and (3) relatively low central bank involvement in holding of deposits (ratio cd). These three characteristics of entropy and leakage of reserve money may be considered consistent with the most differentiated and efficient financial organization in industrial economies to reflect both the institutional structure of the economic system and the highest level of economic development of these economies.

Greater entropy and leakage of reserve money in developing economies reflects the greater demand for reserve money by monetary institutions (ratio e) and greater demand for currency by nonmonetary units (ratio c), which is logical under conditions of less differentiated financial organization and less efficient financial markets. In the oil-exporting economies the large government holdings of deposits by central banks contribute to the highest leakage of reserve money (ratio p) in comparison with all groups of economies.

Lower entropy and leakage of reserve money (ratio p) in socialist decentralized economies than in capitalist economies at the same level of economic development mainly reflect the low holdings as deposits by central banks, which is mainly a result of government regulations that exclude central banks from deposit operations and the low central government deposits with central banks.

Higher ratio p in socialist economies with centralized economic decisionmaking (SCE) nominally reflects greater involvement by central banks in holding deposits of nonmonetary units (ratio d) and relatively high entropy of reserve money (ratio e). The specific statistical features of central bank operations in monobanking systems in these economies have to be observed for a better understanding of these ratios in a comparison with ratios in economies with decentralized economic decisionmaking.

Leakage of money (ratio k) appears to be primarily influenced by (1) the economic development level, (2) balance-of-payments transactions, and (3) institutional structure of the economic system. Their influence is different on two components of leakage of money: leakage of money to nonmonetary deposits with monetary institutions (ratio t) and leakage or creation of money through foreign exchange transactions of monetary institutions (ratio f) .

The greatest leakage of money (the lowest k ratio) in industrial economies evolves from a high leakage of money to nonmonetary deposits, while foreign exchange transactions have the effect of creating money. This is the result of a high savings ratio by nonmonetary units (households) and efficient stimulation by investments to these deposits by the differentiated structure of monetary institutions and favorable balance-of-payments accounts and less sensitivity displayed by monetary institutions to surplus or deficits of current account of balance-of-payments transactions and their influence on creation or withdrawal of money by foreign exchange transactions of monetary institutions. Thus, leakage of money in these countries is the exclusive result of (1) leakage of money in nonmonetary deposits; (2) foreign exchange transactions of monetary institutions contributing to a slight opposite correction in the leakage of money in nonmonetary deposits coming from decentralized economic decisionmaking and from high efficiency of monetary institutions in stimulating these deposits; and (3) the high level of economic development reflected in favorable balance-of-payments accounts.

The low leakage of money in oil-exporting developing economies reflects the influence of favorable balance-of-payments accounts leading to high government incomes from oil exports. This results in a relatively high leakage of money in central government nonmonetary deposits and a higher ratio t than in industrial economies, accompanied by a high level of creation of money by foreign exchange transactions by monetary institutions (ratio f) . This greatly compensates for leakage of money in nonmonetary deposits and leads to relatively low total leakage of money—nearly half that in industrial economies—and a high k ratio.

Lower leakage of money in non–oil-exporting developing capitalist economies is the result of two opposite influences: (1) lower leakage of money to nonmonetary deposits (ratio t); and (2) leakage of money by foreign exchange transactions by monetary institutions, unlike money created by these transactions in industrial economies. This makes leakage of money in these economies less than in industrial economies, although they are greater in oil-exporting developing economies. These causes for the leakage of money in these economies appear logical because of the (1) lower savings ratio by households, (2) less efficient monetary institutions, and (3) deterioration in balance-of-payments transactions.

The leakage of money in socialist decentralized economies, like that found in non–oil-exporting capitalist developing economies, is the result of lower leakage of money to nonmonetary deposits with monetary institutions because there is less activity in these deposits by monetary institutions and a lower savings ratio by households. However, there is a higher leakage of money by foreign exchange transactions from more widespread involvement by monetary institutions in the financing of balance-of-payments current account deficits than in capitalist economies at the same level of economic development.

Lower leakage of money in socialist centralized economies than in socialist decentralized economies, as well as in non–oil-exporting developing capitalist economies, appears to be the result of a lower leakage of money into nonmonetary deposits by monetary institutions as a result of a lower savings ratio by households and lower stimulation of these deposits by monetary institutions. In addition, the lower leakage of money by foreign exchange transactions by monetary institutions than in socialist decentralized economies is the result of very firm control over balance-of-payments transactions, so that lower leakage of money is observable despite broad involvement by monetary institutions in this process.

Leakage of money to nonmonetary deposits by monetary institutions (ratio t) mainly involves leakage of money to quasi-money deposits. However, one part goes to other deposits and liabilities of monetary institutions. The share of this leakage of money to other than quasi-money deposits was greater in industrial (30 percent) than in developing capitalist countries (19 percent). This is a logical reflection of the greater differentiation of these other than quasi-money instruments in industrial countries and greater resources for investments in these instruments in countries with a greater savings ratio by households. The share of leakage of money to other than quasi-money deposits by monetary institutions is lower in socialist than in capitalist countries: 11 percent in decentralized and only 3 percent in centralized socialist countries. A specific case is the oil-exporting countries, where leakage of money to other than quasi-money liabilities of monetary institutions was extremely high (71 percent). These results support the observation that this leakage of money (ratio t) is higher at the maximum level of economic development involving greater diversity in financial institutions and financial instruments and is greater in capitalist rather than socialist economies.

Compared with the stock ratios at the end of 1978, leakage of money to nonmonetary deposits increased in industrial countries from 0.76 percent to 0.82 percent and in oil-exporting developing capitalist countries from 2.01 percent to 2.08 percent. It decreased in non–oil-exporting developing countries from 0.63 percent to 0.52 percent in socialist countries, although more in socialist centralized economies (0.46 percent to 0.31 percent) than in socialist decentralized economies, which explains the slow economic growth and restrictive economic policy.

Leakage (creation) of money by foreign exchange transactions reflects the higher increase in foreign liabilities than in foreign assets of monetary institutions in developing non–oil-exporting countries and socialist countries, while a greater increase in foreign assets than in foreign liabilities of monetary institutions is observable in industrial countries and oil-exporting developing capitalist countries.

In a comparison of leakage (creation) of money by foreign exchange transactions by monetary institutions at the end of 1978, deterioration in foreign markets and balance-of-payments transactions was revealed by a lower creation of money by foreign exchange transactions in 1979 to 1983 than at the end of 1978 in industrial economies and oil-exporting developing capitalist economies. In non–oil-exporting developing capitalist countries, the creation of money by foreign exchange transactions was transformed into leakage of money by these transactions. In socialist economies (centralized and decentralized), leakage of money from foreign exchange transactions increased.

Two subjects related to the structure of reserve money creation should be addressed: the share of domestic and foreign transactions in reserve money creation, and domestic instruments structure of reserve money creation.

In industrial countries and oil-exporting developing capitalist countries, both foreign and domestic instruments represent sources for reserve money creation. In non–oil-exporting capitalist economies and socialist (centralized and decentralized) economies, domestic instruments represent the only instruments for reserve money creation; in both cases foreign exchange transactions by central banks represent instruments of reserve money creation/withdrawal. Thus, foreign exchange transactions of monetary institutions had the same impact on creation/withdrawal of reserve money as they had on creation/leakage of money supply.

The domestic instruments structure in reserve money creation differs among countries because of different (1) institutional economic systems, (2) economic development levels, and (3) exogenous influences. In industrial countries, the main source for reserve money creation was from central bank financing of the central government $(_cA_g)$, and the second most important source was from central bank crediting of monetary institutions $(_cA_m)$. Extraordinary financial transactions by central banks $(_cU_a)$ were not used as instruments for reserve money creation.

A similar structure for reserve money creation by domestic instruments is observed in developing non–oil-exporting economies, although extraordinary central bank transactions appear as the third significant source, with central bank crediting of nonmonetary units as the least significant vehicle for reserve money creation.

In developing oil-exporting capitalist economies, the main sources for reserve money creation were (1) extraordinary central bank transactions, (2) central bank crediting of monetary institutions, and (3) central bank crediting of the central government.

In socialist decentralized economies, the main source for reserve money creation was central bank crediting of the central government, which occurs in industrial economies and developing non–oil-exporting capitalist economies. However, the second important source in reserve money creation was effected through central bank transactions, while the third was through central bank crediting of monetary institutions, with the least important being central bank crediting of nonmonetary units.

In socialist centralized economies, the specific financial organization was reflected in central bank crediting of nonmonetary units (socialist enterprises) as the main source for reserve money creation, while the second was central bank crediting of monetary institutions. The third was central bank crediting of the central government, with the least important being central bank transactions.

A comparison of the stock structure of reserve money creation with that at the end of 1978 shows changes in this structure that predominantly reflect a deterioration in balance-of-payments accounts. Empirical evidence shows that foreign exchange transactions by monetary institutions in industrial economies and developing oil-exporting economies remain the source for reserve money creation in similar shares in total reserve money creation (3 percent less in industrial economies and 4 percent more in developing oil-exporting economies than at the end of 1978). A deterioration of balance-of-payments accounts has significantly affected the impact of foreign exchange transactions on reserve money creation in developing non–oil-exporting capitalist economies and socialist decentralized economies. The result was a transformation of foreign exchange transactions on monetary institutions in developing non–oil-exporting economies from an instrument of creation at the end of 1978 to an instrument for the withdrawal of reserve money in 1979–83 (16 percent creation at the end of 1978, 136 percent withdrawal in 1979–83 of total created reserve money). In socialist decentralized economies, there was a sharp increase in withdrawal of reserve money by foreign exchange transactions by monetary institutions, from 10 percent at the end of 1978 to 368 percent of total created reserve money in 1979–83. Finally, there were no significant ill effects from a deterioration in balance-of-payments transactions in socialist centralized economies, mainly because of strong government control exerted over these transactions to decrease the withdrawal of reserve money by the foreign exchange transactions of monetary institutions from 29 percent of total created reserve money at the end of 1978 to 12 percent in 1979–83.

Different changes in the domestic instruments structure of reserve money creation are observed in the structure of these instruments at the end of 1978. Here again, there were no significant changes in the instrument structure in industrial countries, similar to the stability from foreign exchange transactions on reserve money creation, and in socialist centralized countries from similar regulations. The most significant changes are observed in other groups of countries in transactions by central banks ($_cU_a$). Consistent with the deterioration in the balance-of-payments position of non–oil-exporting economies and increased central bank support of a restrictive economic policy, these transactions became a significant source for reserve money creation compared with their negligible role at the end of 1978.

The same change has arisen in socialist decentralized economies, where transactions by central banks became the second important source for reserve money creation. In oil-exporting developing capitalist economies, central bank transactions became the main source for reserve money creation to replace central bank crediting by the central government at the end of 1978.

However, the most stable share in reserve money creation by domestic instruments is observed in central bank crediting of the central government. This retained the same share in the structure for all groups of countries, except oil-exporting developing capitalist countries. It remained the most important source for reserve money creation in (1) industrial economies, (2) non–oil-exporting developing capitalist economies, and (3) socialist decentralized economies, and the third most important in socialist centralized economies. Similar stability in the share of reserve money creation by domestic instruments is apparent in the central bank credits to monetary institutions—the only exception being socialist decentralized economies—as the second important source for reserve money creation.

The above analysis of the reserve money structure suggests that events related to the institutional economic system and the level of economic development have influenced the structure of the creation of reserve money. From 1979 to 1983, and at the end of 1978, the central deviations of the creation of reserve money mainly reflect the shocks from a deterioration in balance-of-payments transactions, the accompanying slowdown of economic development, and restrictive economic policies.

Some varieties of change in the reserve money structure from 1979 to 1983, compared with the creation of money structure at the end of 1978, may be observed at different levels of economic development in developing economies. However, they do not impact on the basic content of the assessments of changes in the creation of reserve money structure in this period.

9

The Influence of Balance of Payments on the Money Supply Process

A holistic and structural comparative analysis of the MSP has shown that foreign exchange transactions by monetary institutions have had a significant influence on the MSP, especially in countries at a lower level of economic development with decentralized economic decisionmaking. Because of the dramatic impact of balance-of-payments transactions, surplus, deficits in current accounts, and foreign exchange transactions by monetary institutions on the money supply process, this chapter will be devoted to an explanation of this influential process. This is initially important because (1) there is no direct influence of balance-of-payments transactions on the MSP; and (2) there are great changes in current accounts of balance-of-payments transactions in developing countries that indirectly influence foreign exchange transactions by monetary institutions, and in this way influence monetary multipliers and the creation of reserve money structure. In view of the flow nature of balance-of-payments transactions, only the flow aspect of the MSP is analyzed here for 1979–83.

The influence of the balance of payments on the MSP occurs through two different channels: (1) current account surplus or deficit; and (2) the involvement of monetary institutions in foreign financial transactions in balance of payments parallel with the involvement of nonmonetary units in these transactions. It is logical to expect that a surplus of current account of balance of payments leads to the creation of money and reserve money with the opposite effect for a current account deficit. The second group of influences on the MSP may modify the impact of balance of payments on the MSP—even totally eliminate it—so that foreign exchange transactions by monetary institutions have an effect on monetary multipliers and the reserve money creation structure opposite to that logically expected from the surplus or deficit of balance-of-payments current account. In this way, a surplus or deficit of current account balance of payments appears as an indirect source of influence on the MSP, while foreign exchange transactions by monetary institutions partly reflect their involvement in foreign financing representing the direct influence on the MSP. Consequently, this second source of balance-of-payments influence on the MSP becomes more significant than the first.

There are three groups of foreign exchange transactions by monetary institutions: (1) foreign exchange transactions with foreign residents; (2) foreign exchange transactions by monetary institutions with domestic residents; (3) semiforeign exchange and semidomestic transactions by monetary institutions with domestic residents (buying/selling of foreign exchange for domestic currency) that involve different types of buying/selling of foreign exchange between monetary authorities, other monetary institutions, and nonmonetary units. It may be concluded that the first two groups of transactions do not have a direct effect on the MSP, so that the monetary effects of balance-of-payments transactions and related foreign exchange transactions are accomplished by the third group: buying/selling of foreign exchange between central banks and other monetary institutions for domestic currency, influencing the amount of creation/withdrawal of reserve money ($_cE_n$). The buying/selling of foreign exchange between monetary institutions and nonmonetary units for domestic currency influences the amount of creation or leakage of money in circulation (E_n) or reserve money ($_cE_n$).

The influence of balance-of-payments transactions on the MSP reflects the effects of a combination of buying/selling of foreign exchange instruments for domestic currency, with central banks and other monetary institutions and nonmonetary units as buyers and sellers. These transactions mirror the net changes in foreign assets and foreign liabilities in monetary institutions impacting on money supply, foreign assets, and liabilities in the central banking system influencing reserve money.[1]

Based on this interpretation of the influence of balance-of-payments transactions on the MSP, two groups of questions need to undergo an empirical investigation: (1) the influence of balance-of-payments transactions on the MSP, as reflected in the number of countries obviously under the influence of balance-of-payments transactions (their share in the total number of countries involved in a group); and (2) the interrelationship between balance-of-payments transactions and monetary multipliers, their ratios, and the creation of reserve money by groups of countries classified by institutional economic systems and economic development levels.[2]

An investigation of the first question is based on ratios presenting relationships between amount of leakage/creation of money from foreign exchange transactions by monetary institutions (E_n) and amounts of creation/withdrawal of reserve money by these transactions ($_cE_n$), along with the amounts and signs of the current account of balance of payments (surplus or deficit). The positive signs of these ratios indicate the logically expected influence of balance of payments on the quantity of money and reserve money, while negative signs indicate that the logically expected influence cannot be observed at this time. The positive ratios in total number of cases indicate the degree of this influence. Four varieties of influences on the MSP in balance of payments emerge: (1) positive signs of both E_n and $_cE_n$ to balance-of-payments current account surplus or deficit; (2) positive sign only in E_n; (3) positive sign only in $_cE_n$; and (4) no positive signs (current account deficit accompanied by creation of money and reserve money, and current account surplus accompanied by leakage of money and withdrawal of reserve money). Case (1) indicates the logical influence of balance of payments on both creation of money and reserve money. Cases (2) and (3) mean that this influence is observed in only creation of money (2) or creation of reserve money. Cases (3) and (4) indicate that the influence of the balance of payments on the MSP is not apparent, with empirical evidence indicating an opposite effect of foreign exchange transactions by monetary institutions.

Using the empirical evidence on these ratios, the conclusion is that balance-of-payments transactions have a greater influence in countries at a lower level of economic development and countries with a lower degree of decentralization in economic decisionmaking. The full influence of balance of payments on the MSP (positive sign in both E_n and $_cE_n$ ratios to balance-of-payments current account surplus or deficit) is observed primarily in socialist centralized countries (100 percent), and in socialist decentralized countries (close to 100 percent). In capitalist countries, this influence is noticeable in more non–oil-exporting developing economies (60 percent), while only 21 percent of industrial countries have an MSP influenced by balance of payments. Consistent with this is the empirical evidence on countries with no influence of balance of payments (negative signs in ratios of both E_n and $_cE_n$ to deficit or surplus of current account of balance of payments). No such countries have socialist economies (centralized or decentralized); the lion's share belongs to the industrial countries (42 percent), although 27 percent are non–oil-exporting developing countries. A similar situation arises in one positive ratio (E_n or cE_n) to surplus or deficit of balance-of-payments current account.

In this way, empirical evidence proves the logical expectation that the influence of balance of payments on the MSP is lower in economies where nonmonetary units are more involved in foreign financial transactions. Thus, the relatively low influence of balance of payments on the MSP in industrial countries reflects greater involvement by exporters and importers in foreign financial transactions. Contrary to this, the relatively lower direct involvement of exporters and importers in financing balance-of-payments transactions in non–oil-exporting developing economies means greater involvement by monetary institutions in the financing of these transactions, resulting in a greater influence on balance-of-payments transactions in these countries. Little or no financing of balance-of-payments transactions by nonmonetary units logically reflects the almost complete influence of balance-of-payments transactions on the MSP in socialist countries with decentralized and centralized economic decisionmaking.

These conclusions about the influence of balance-of-payments transactions on the MSP in developing capitalist non–oil-exporting economies and socialist economies are based only on deficit current accounts of balance of payments. Powerful balance-of-payments transactions can again be expected in surplus current accounts. Support for this conclusion is found in the creation of money and reserve money, with the significantly less withdrawal and leakage of money and reserve money observed at the end of 1978, which reflects the more favorable balance-of-payments current accounts in developing economies and socialist economies.

The interrelationship between surplus or deficit of current account balance of payments, monetary multipliers, their ratios, and the creation of reserve money is analyzed here, with its focus on the conclusions about relationships of institutional economic systems and levels of economic development. We investigate relationships within a framework of creation or withdrawal of reserve money by foreign exchange transactions (cE_n) and creation or leakage of money (E_n).

There is no direct influence of the balance-of-payments current account amount on these variables (cE_n and E_n), which are ultimately influenced by foreign exchange transactions in the buying/selling of foreign exchange for domestic currency between central banks and other monetary institutions—and between monetary institutions and nonmonetary units. Therefore, ratios presenting relationships between these variables (cE_n, E_n) and surplus or deficit amounts of current accounts of balance of payments indicate deviations in these variables, i.e., the final effects of foreign exchange transactions on the MSP may deviate from deficit or surplus amounts of current account of balance of payments as a result of their deviations from domestic foreign exchange and semiforeign exchange transactions of monetary institutions. The observed ratios indicate how much balance-of-payments transactions can be considered as a source of influence on the MSP in countries with different institutional economic systems and levels of economic development. Ratios lower than 1.0 indicate the degree of the reduction in balance-of-payments transactions influence on the MSP and domestic foreign exchange transactions. A specific case represents ratios greater than 1.0 in some groups of countries that indicate a more significant impact on foreign exchange transactions on the MSP than is found in balance-of-payments transactions.

In countries with positive signs of $_cE_n$ and E_n ratios to surplus or deficit of current account of balance of payments, these conclusions appear:

1. In capitalist industrial countries, balance-of-payments transactions are not as pronounced in creation/withdrawal of reserve money ($_cE_n$), as in non–oil-exporting developing countries. Higher ratios in these developing countries reflect greater involvement by central banks in foreign financing, and banks in domestic buying/selling of foreign exchange for domestic currency. Wide differences in these ratios in individual groups of these countries reflect the broad spectrum of the involvement of central banks in these transactions, which includes a group of countries with a greater creation/withdrawal of reserve money from the foreign exchange transactions by central banks than the current account of their balance of payments. Oil-exporting countries are similar to industrial countries in creation/withdrawal of reserve money with balance-of-payments transactions—primarily reflecting broad involvement by the central government in balance-of-payments transactions in using the surplus of current account of these transactions.

In the relationship between creation/leakage of money (E_n) and balance-of-payments transactions, ratios indicate relatively smaller differences among countries involved, suggesting that less involvement by central banks in foreign exchange transactions is significantly corrected by greater involvement by other monetary institutions in these transactions. The exceptions are countries at the lowest development level, and oil-exporting countries. These ratios are greater than 1.0, which indicates a more far-reaching influence by foreign exchange transactions on the MSP than the amount of current account of balance of payments under study; however, the exception is oil-exporting countries and non–oil-exporting developing countries at the lowest level of economic development. This primarily indicates the influence of extraordinary changes in foreign markets and balance-of-payments transactions.

2. In socialist economies with decentralized economic decisionmaking, the striking feature about these ratios is the differences between the groups of countries at the highest level of economic development and the other two groups at lower levels of economic development, which indicate that different regulations relevant for balance-of-payments and foreign exchange transactions are important. With the small number of countries involved in these groups, it is difficult to use this empirical evidence as a basis for some general conclusions on relationships to balance-of-payments transactions within these countries or in comparison with other institutional economic systems.

3. In socialist economies with centralized economic decisionmaking, only two countries are involved in this analysis, making general conclusions difficult. Within this framework of empirical evidence, two characteristics of the balance-of-payments relationship to creation or withdrawal of reserve money ($_cE_n$) and to creation or leakage of money (E_n) appear. Both relationships are lower than in capitalist countries and in socialist countries with decentralized economic decisionmaking; and ratios related to $_cE_n$ are similar to those related to the foreign exchange transactions of other monetary institutions, so the ratio related to E_n is nearly twice as great as the $_cE_n$ ratio.

Our general conclusion is that the empirical evidence on the influence of balance-of-payments transactions on the MSP proves the hypothesis on the significant role of balance-of-payments transactions as exogenous sources strongly influencing the MSP during this period of deteriorating foreign markets and balance of payments by individual countries. In the complex relationship of balance-of-payments transactions with the MSP, direct and indirect influences should be noted separately. The indirect effects of the buying/selling of foreign exchange among monetary and nonmonetary entities appear stronger than the direct effects.

Two groups of influences on the balance-of-payments transactions should be distinguished: (a) surplus or deficit of current account of balance of payments, and (b) the specific structure of foreign exchange transactions by monetary and nonmonetary entities for balance-of-payments transactions. Both of these influences on the MSP differ by institutional economic systems and economic development levels by individual country. Repercussions from a surplus/deficit of current account of balance-of-payments surface in developing economies, both capitalist and socialist (centralized and decentralized), because of the dominant effect of deteriorated foreign markets on balance-of-payments transactions. Reaction to balance-of-payments transactions and to foreign exchange transactions related to balance-of-payments transactions on the MSP are stronger in developing capitalist and socialist economies. This reflects broader involvement by monetary institutions in foreign financial transactions and less by nonmonetary entities than in developed countries.

Thus, these two groups of influences on balance of payments on the MSP prove the hypothesis that the exogenous influence of balance-of-payments transactions on the MSP should be greater in capitalist developing economies and socialist economies due to greater involvement of monetary institutions in foreign financial transactions and their greater sensitivity to a deterioration in foreign markets.

NOTES

1. In an interpretation of the empirical evidence on foreign exchange transactions by monetary institutions dealing with domestic nonmonetary entities, the need to modify the evidence has arisen. This is explained in "A Guide to Money and Banking Statistics," *International Financial Statistics* (1984): "The terms governing foreign currency transactions between financial institutions and residents are often subject to statutory provisions on the assignment of local currency values that may differ from the booking rates for foreign currency items relating to nonresidents" (paragraph 221). Also, "In practice, it has rarely been possible to implement the preferred conversion practices for foreign currency items when national practices differ from the IFS standard" (paragraph 223). As a specific case about the modification of the value of foreign exchange transactions represents the practice of governments to impose additional charges or premiums related to buying/selling of foreign exchange by residents, or use of separate exchange rates in buying/selling of foreign exchange by residents.

2. The empirical evidence on current accounts of balance of payments by individual countries in this analysis is taken from the *International Financial Statistics*, with data presented in U.S. dollars, which are transformed to domestic currency data by applying the average exchange rates of national currencies in lines "rf" or "rh" on country pages in the *International Financial Statistics*. However, this evidence is not available for all countries in this analysis, causing the number of countries included to be less than the total number of countries.

10

The Influence of Institutional Sectors on the Money Supply Process

The MSP is influenced not only by the central banking system (monetary authorities) but also by other institutional sectors, including other monetary institutions, nonmonetary units (domestic/foreign and financial/nonfinancial). This approach is particularly significant in a comparative analysis of the MSP because of the variations in the role of individual institutional sectors in national economies at different levels of economic development and different economic systems. Conclusions will be based on a holistic and structural analysis.

According to the basic formula of the MSP in this analysis ($M = {}_cA \cdot m$), the role of institutional sectors in the MSP should be investigated separately covering two avenues: (1) creation/withdrawal of reserve money (${}_cA$), and (2) monetary multipliers. Conclusions based on a logical analysis of the role of institutional sectors in the MSP, and the empirical analysis whenever possible, are the two approaches to these problems. Analysis should investigate which institutional sectors can influence the size and changes in ratios determining monetary multipliers and the structure of reserve money creation. Empirical analysis should investigate how these influences are reflected in statistical evidence by logical analysis and an interpretation of the empirical evidence built upon a previous explanation of the nature of these influences to understand macrotargets and the behavior of the central banking system, micromotivation, and the behavior of other institutional sectors in the MSP.

Conclusions based on explanations in this book appear significant and relevant for a comparative empirical analysis of the role of institutional sectors in the MSP. The central banking system (monetary authorities) exerts strong control over reserve money creation ($_cA$) or maximum amount of reserve money as a part of monetary planning and the implementation of monetary policy targets. Significant modifications in the targets of the decisionmaking power of the central banking system in reserve money creation and implementation may come from central government influence (direct or indirect). Other institutional sectors may have a significant influence if their demand for reserve money proves lower than what the central banking system offers. Government influence on the creation of reserve money and amount by the central banking system may be considered as highly important, while the second source of influence is theoretical in nature, not readily obvious. The logical conclusion is that the central banking system is able to control reserve money creation, but its ability may be reduced by central government influence in countries where this influence is institutionalized. This government influence is not empirically apparent, so the logical conclusion about the firm control over reserve money by the central banking system cannot be empirically investigated. The power to control the central banking system is far less in monetary multipliers.

The size of the monetary multiplier is influenced by all institutional sectors involved in monetary transactions (see equations 8 and 9 in chapter 1 involving variables and ratios). All sectors influence ratio k, which involves variables and ratios related to the creation and leakage of money: (1) total amount of investments by monetary institutions (A), (2) total amount of nonmonetary deposits and other nonmonetary investments of nonmonetary subjects in monetary institutions (T) less net foreign assets of monetary institutions (E_n). Ratio k is then influenced by nonmonetary subjects impacting variables (A), (T), and (E_n) by the central banking system, which, in turn, influences other monetary institutions and the rest of the world in balance of payments and E_n. However, ratio k of the monetary multiplier reflects the influence of all institutional sectors involving the influence of individual institutional sectors on individual variables not empirically apparent from the institutional sectors that cannot be empirically analyzed.

In ratio p representing the denominator of the formula defining monetary multipliers, four variables are involved: (1) leakage of reserve money in currency in circulation (C), (2) entropy of reserve money (R), (3) monetary deposits with the central banking system ($_cDM$), and (4) nonmonetary deposits and other investments in the central banking system (cT). Leakage of reserve money in currency in circulation is fully dependent on nonmonetary subjects. Entropy of reserve money (R) is partly dependent on the reserve requirement ratio from the central banking system and on other monetary institutions, with their assessment of the higher demand for this money. We may assume that the reserve requirement ratio determines that part of reserve money on accounts from other monetary institutions with the central banking system that is not available for current transactions by these institutions; consequently, according to liquidity policies, additional amounts of reserve money on these accounts for current payments must be held. The other two ratios (cDM and cT) depend primarily on regulations on obligatory deposits with the central banking system. Data on the amounts of these variables cannot be used as evidence for the influence of institutional sectors on leakage of reserve money. An empirical analysis of the impact of institutional sectors on ratio p can be applied to entropy of reserve money (ratio e) and leakage of reserve money in currency in circulation (ratio c). Thus, only these two ratios are empirically analyzed here.

In addition to limitations on empirical analysis of the influence of institutional sectors on monetary multipliers on only two variables and their ratios, we should address the influence of other institutional sectors, which are micromotivated, neglecting macrotargets of monetary policy and the macroconcept of the MSP. Empirical evidence on other monetary institutions and nonmonetary subjects on these two ratios does not focus on their power but rather on the impact of their micromotivation and the behavior of these ratios and monetary multipliers, which differs from the macrobehavior of the central banking system.

For the comparative empirical analysis of the influence of other monetary institutions on entropy of reserve money (ratio e), the quotient of ratio e to ratio p is used to indicate the share of entropy of reserve money (e) in total amount of reserve money, i.e., in the sum of all ratios involved in the denominator of equation 9. The greater this quotient, the greater the role of entropy of reserve money in monetary multiplication and the role of other monetary institutions to determine the size of the monetary multiplier. Empirical evidence (as of late 1978) shows that this $e{:}p$ quotient in capitalist countries is larger in industrial countries than in developing countries, and larger in developing countries at higher levels of economic development; however, it is lower in socialist decentralized economies than in capitalist economies but at a higher degree in economic development within these economies. The highest value of this quotient is in socialist centralized economies, but it is difficult to compare it with other groups of economies because of the differences in presentation of central bank transactions.

This comparative size of the $e:p$ quotient by groups of countries appears contradictory to comparative size of ratio e by groups of countries, where the greater ratio e at a lower level of economic development is observable. The explanation is that quotient $e:p$ represents the relative value of ratio e, i.e., the share of ratio e in ratio p, so that the value of quotient $e:p$ depends not only on the size of ratio e but also on the size of other components of ratio p. We may then conclude that ratio e is relatively lower in industrial than in developing economies (higher at a lower level of economic development). However, the opposite rule is shown in other components of ratio p. Thus, the greater size of quotient $e:p$, indicating a greater share of ratio e in ratio p, and being a more important determinant of ratio p, proves to be a better indicator of the role of other monetary institutions in monetary multiplication than the size of ratio e. Thus, the empirical evidence proves the greater influence of other monetary institutions on monetary multipliers in capitalist than in socialist countries. Similar conclusions are valid for the MSP in 1979 to 1983. These relationships, however, appear reversed at the end of 1983 because of a rise in extraordinary transactions by central banks in their function to create reserve money within a framework of foreign and domestic economic development.

Representing the share of leakage of reserve money in currency in circulation through nonmonetary subjects, the quotient $c:p$ indicates the influence of nonmonetary subjects on ratio p and the monetary multiplier. The empirical evidence reveals that this influence is greater than entropy of reserve money (greater quotient $c:p$ than $e:p$), which indicates greater autonomous influence of nonmonetary entities on ratio p than the autonomous influence of monetary institutions. This means that ratio p is strongly influenced by the autonomous behavior of economic units, not only by the behavior of other monetary institutions presented in quotient $e:p$ but also in the autonomous behavior of nonmonetary units presented in quotient $c:p$.

Empirical evidence shows that this autonomous influence of nonmonetary units on ratio p is most pronounced in socialist decentralized economies but lowest in socialist centralized economies. In capitalist economies it is highest in industrial countries—contrary to the lowest ratio c in these economies—because of lower influence by other components of ratio p similar to quotient $e:p$ in these economies. The rule of increasing order of quotient $e:p$ following increasing order of the level of economic development of developing economies (late 1978 and

1979–83 flows) is not shown in quotient $c:p$. The empirical evidence proves the increasing order of this quotient following a decrease in the economic development level. The rule in quotient $e:p$ is observed in a lower degree of increasing order of quotient $c:p$, more in the case of ratio c. The main reason for this difference is the low share of monetary and other deposits by nonmonetary units with the central banking system (ratios d and $_ct$) in socialist decentralized economies and their decrease in this period.

The lowest quotient $c:p$ and its stability in socialist centralized economies reflects the specific liability structure of the central bank under the monobanking system, which cannot be compared with this quotient in economies with decentralized economic decisionmaking and decentralized financial structure.

The relative size of ratio c (quotient $c:p$) indicates the significant autonomous influence of nonmonetary units on the MSP through their behavior in holding currency in circulation. Significant changes in the absolute and relative size of this ratio indicate significant influence of these units on changes in ratio p and the monetary multipliers. However, this is only an indication that nonmonetary units exercise influence through holding currency. If other, empirically nonidentifiable means of influence on nonmonetary units on the MSP are considered, their impact is greater when observed from the absolute and relative size of ratio c, which reflects currency held by these units.

The behavior of institutional sectors in the demand for money, particularly in the readiness of the individual institutional sectors to hold extra quantities of money for a long time or beyond demand for money is very significant in a comparative analysis of the monetary processes, including the MSP. These "residual institutional sectors" in demand for money may differ by economic systems, which contribute to wider differences in the MSP and other monetary processes in economies with different institutional economic systems. As a rule, the behavior of an economic subject depends primarily on its profit motivation and sensitivity, which vary with its extra money holdings. This is mainly true of governments in all economic systems. In socialist economies, it appears reasonable to assume a low level of sensitivity to extra money holdings by socialist enterprises, especially in socialist enterprises in centralized socialist economies—the behavior of socialist enterprises making money on their accounts. This is also true of socialist enterprises in decentralized socialist economies, with a lower profit motivation, along with public ownership enterprises in capitalist economies. The impact of this behavior of the institutional sectors on the MSP and the specific characteristics of the institutional sectors in different institutional economic systems are reservoirs for the differences in monetary multipliers and their relevant ratios.

This analysis of the forces impacting on institutional sectors in the MSP is also an analysis of the controllability of the MSP by the central banking system and the role of autonomous influences on it. Therefore, we may conclude that, first, the central banking system has efficient control over creation of reserve money (cA), if not disturbed by government influence. Its power to control the monetary multiplier is far weaker, usually in controlling a minimal amount of reserve money on accounts of monetary institutions with the central banking system (reserve requirement ratio), i.e., control over minimal entropy of reserve money (ratio e).

Second, the other institutional sectors, other monetary institutions, and nonmonetary entities have a significant influence on monetary multipliers to influence both basic ratio k and basic ratio p by their micromotivated behavior from their portfolio selection decisionmaking. A significant autonomous influence on monetary multiplication is to be assumed based on micromotivated behavior that may not be consistent with the macrogoals and targets of the central banking system policy and economic policy.

Third, the degree of controllability of the MSP and the ability of monetary policy to implement one of its basic targets may appear modest with monetary policy as one of the main instruments of economic policy. However, the influence of the central banking system on the MSP dominates, with the central banking system in control of the MSP and its final outcome: changes in the money supply.

This conclusion is based on the ability of the central banking system to control reserve money creation (cA) and to adjust this amount to reflect a minimal demand for money and credit by nonmonetary entities, assuming the behavior of nonmonetary entities is properly investigated and perceived. Then, the central banking system can influence monetary multiplication not only through the reserve requirements ratio but through the behavior of other monetary institutions, nonmonetary entities (indirectly), interest rate policies, and foreign exchange policy, which are supported by government fiscal policy. Finally, direct control measures for investments by other monetary institutions, extraordinary measures for obligatory deposits by other monetary institutions, and nonmonetary entities with the central banking system can influence the monetary multiplication process and the size of monetary multipliers.

11

Summary of Conclusions

The process of creating money is crucial to monetary theory and monetary practice. It has been traditionally interpreted in a specific environment of highly developed capitalist economies and under very specific assumptions about conclusions on its analysis. Often these conclusions were oversimplified and inapplicable to most of the differentiated economic structures in institutional economic systems and economic development levels. This is important, for it reveals what happens when we ignore differences between highly developed capitalist economies and other broad economic structures in money supply control, which represent a basic target for monetary and financial policy in less developed economies.

The general theory of the MSP, neither general monetary theory nor financial theory, is applicable in a world environment of differentiated types of economies, which imposes the need to reinvestigate the existing theory of the MSP, general monetary theory, financial theories, and creative theories within a framework of the existing economies with different economic systems at different levels of economic development. The goal to create a general theory on the MSP, which is applicable to all economies, may appear ambitious for this study because of missing general monetary and financial theories related to the MSP. However, if the attempt to reach this goal does not prove fully successful, it does mean a significant contribution to an understanding of the need for a reinvestigation of existing stringent monetary and financial theories and the creation of general theories to be adjusted to institutional and economic environments in the existing differentiated economic structure.

The main highway leading to these goals is a comparative analysis of economies with all types of institutional economic systems and economic development levels. The treasure trove of comparative statistical information published by the International Monetary Fund has made it possible to organize such an analysis in this book to include one hundred countries with different institutional economic systems (capitalist, socialist with decentralized economic decisionmaking, and socialist with centralized economic decisionmaking) at different levels of economic development. These range from those countries at the highest level of economic development, or industrial countries, to those at the lowest level of economic development—below $360 per capita GNP. To our knowledge, this is the first attempt at global comparative study in money and finance. Although it cannot be expected to present final conclusions, it may at least present a fresh perspective to comparative studies in monetary and financial fields.

This study is designed to define conclusions about the differences in the MSP in different types of economies, the reasons for these differences, and the general rules for all types of economies based on a theoretical framework of wealth-approach and portfolio utility optimalization theories. We consider the MSP a part of the broad financial/nonfinancial transactions structure. This framework includes both monetary institutions (central banks and other monetary institutions) and nonmonetary entities (domestic and foreign).

Within the transactions/transactor structure, the highly relative nature of the MSP, with its dependence on the institutional economic system and economic development level, is influenced by the general health of the economy at that time. This comparative study of the MSP is based on the hypothesis that the differences are caused by national economies related to the institutional economic system and economic development level. In addition to these endogenous factors, some exogenous influences must be considered, with their impact on significant modifications to these endogenous factors related to a deterioration in foreign markets, balance of payments, and domestic economic developments in many countries after the second increase in oil prices.

A significant aspect of the theoretical approach is that it must respect the needs of monetary practice to offer conclusions contributing to a better understanding of the monetary practice in different types of economies; optimal ways to improve existing monetary institutions, instruments, and practice in national economies; improvements in international financing; and international financial institutions. We applied both static (stock) (as of late 1978 and 1983) and dynamic (flow) (1979–83) approaches in an "interspacial" and "intertemporal" comparative analysis of the MSP. The classification of variables and their ratios was adjusted to (1) leakage, (2) entropy of money and reserve money, (3) complexity (complex, basic, and explanatory variables, and ratios), and (4) the relationship of variables and their ratios to the institutional sectors. In this approach, the basic equation used in this study $(M = c\!A \cdot m)$ includes two main groups of variables and their ratios: (1) creation of reserve money $(c\!A)$ fully controlled by monetary authorities, and (2) monetary multiplier m for variables and ratios partially controlled by monetary authorities and partially influenced by the autonomous behavior of other institutional sectors (monetary/nonmonetary and domestic/foreign).

Based on this approach, the comparative analysis of the MSP is related to the definition of money in a narrow sense (M_1), as applied by the International Monetary Fund in the *International Financial Statistics*. However, the methodology of analysis and conclusions are applicable, *mutatis mutandis*, to broader definitions of money. The equations used to analyze the monetary multiplier can be used for other types of multipliers, e.g., the credit multiplier $(A:c\!A)$.

The definitions of variables are necessarily consistent with those in the *International Financial Statistics*; however, complex variables are defined by comparative analysis needs that impose broader concepts applicable in different types of economies. This is particularly valid for the definition of reserve money—defined as the total amount of central bank investments minus the amount of foreign liabilities.

The methodological approach, which is adjusted to this theoretical approach, includes a two-dimensional matrix classification of the countries involved: horizontal (institutional economic systems) and vertical (economic development levels). There are three basic types of institutional economic systems: capitalist, socialist decentralized, and socialist centralized. There are four levels of economic development, plus a specific group of oil-exporting developing economies. The matrix classification of these economies includes fifteen cells or groups of economies with the same institutional sector and economic development level. The statistical background for a comparative study in these classified economies is the flow-of-funds matrices—prepared for each economy— in a statistical presentation on the country pages of the *International Financial Statistics*. Using this empirical evidence, this comparative analysis involves (1) a definition of the hypothesis of the influence of the institutional sector and level of economic development, and (2) their modifications by exogenous causes. We use empirical evidence to test this hypothesis and to define final conclusions. This analysis is based on a mathematical presentation of national economies, which has been adjusted for comparative analysis (structure and definition of variables and their ratios). However, mathematical methods are not applied in a comparative analysis because it is impossible to quantify two classification criteria, the institutional system and economic development level, in order to present relevant ratios dependent on these two variables.

An empirical comparative analysis of the MSP, presented in two parts, involves two approaches. The first part presents a holistic analysis of the MSP through explanations of the basic relevant characteristics of the individual groups of these economies that have been classified by institutional sector and economic development level (groups of economies within individual cells of the matrix of classification of economies). In addition, the holistic analysis is designed to explain the dispersion of the creation of reserve money, monetary multipliers, and their relevant ratios within these groups of economies (size and causes of dispersion). The arithmetic mean to measure dispersion of the central tendency and standard deviation and range are used. In all phases, the thrust of this analysis is adjusted to structural analysis of the MSP. The second part, the structural comparative analysis of the MSP, is designed to test the hypothesis on the role of institutional economic systems, economic development levels, and exogenous sources on the MSP. This empirical comparative analysis presents final conclusions designed to answer the basic questions of this study.

HOLISTIC ANALYSIS

The holistic analysis shows significant common characteristics of the MSP in groups of economies classified by institutional economic system and economic development level, which is consistent with the hypothesis on their role. Significant dispersion of the creation of reserve money, monetary multipliers, and their relevant ratios is observed in individual groups of economies. This suggests the important influence of exogenous factors, along with the hypothesized influence of endogenous factors (the institutional economic system and economic development level), especially in deteriorating balance-of-payments transactions, domestic economic developments, and increased direct government intervention.

Empirical evidence in a holistic analysis proves the hypothesis on the roles of the institutional economic system and economic development level, and the hypothesis that exogenous influences on the MSP could be important. This conclusion is particularly significant for an interpretation of the empirical evidence in a structural analysis of the MSP, which suggests that we should interpret deviations in the creation of reserve money, monetary multipliers, and their ratios from the hypothesis as the results of parallel influences from exogenous factors, institutional systems, and economic development rather than disapprove the hypothesized role of the institutional economic system and economic development level. This is important to consider because of the exceptionally strong influence of deteriorated foreign and domestic economic developments and a related increase in direct government economic interventions after the second increase in oil prices in 1979.

An interpretation of the empirical evidence in a structural comparative analysis of the MSP is significant in that holistic analysis suggests a differentiation in the two groups of influences on the MSP: (1) economic and (2) regulatory. It also suggests a differentiation of direct and indirect influences, including the interdependence of sources of influence. Several conclusions about a holistic analysis appear significant:

1. The main economic factors influencing the MSP appear on an economic development level in the relevant behavior of economic units through (1) the institutional economic system, (2) the increasing order of decentralization, (3) freedom to make economic decisions, and (4) emphasis on the importance of economic development. Empirical evidence shows the more active role of economic development in capitalist rather than socialist decentralized economies, with its noticeably more active role in decentralized rather than centralized socialist economies. In addition, the level of economic development has had a strong indirect effect on the MSP by its influence on differentiation and the function of the financial structure through less differentiation and efficiency in monetary and financial organizations in developing economies, as compared with those in industrial economies. This indirect influence at the economic development level explains some of the most contradictory behavior of monetary multipliers in capitalist economies, as observed in the structural analysis. This reveals, on an economic development level, only two levels of efficiency and differentiation in the financial structure and corresponding basic levels of monetary multipliers: industrial countries or developed economies, and developing economies. The combined effect of direct and indirect influences of the economic development level on MSP appears to be a greater sensitivity to developing economies in exogenous influences, especially in deteriorating for-

eign markets, which is strengthened by greater involvement by less differentiated monetary/financial organization in foreign and domestic financing; consequently, the impact of the level of economic development on the MSP is more pronounced in these countries.

2. The institutional economic system affects the MSP indirectly through economic development levels, although its direct presence is revealed in socialist countries in the monetary institutions and the use of direct government economic intervention.

3. Exogenous influences on the MSP have a greater impact in the more decentralized economic systems at a lower level of economic development. These influences prove to be the most significant in capitalist countries and socialist decentralized countries and least so in socialist centralized countries, and are stronger at lower rather than higher levels of economic development.

4. The oil-exporting developing countries appear as a specific group, with characteristics in common with both industrial countries (higher per capita GNP and successful balance-of-payments transactions) and developing countries (less differentiated and efficient financial structure and less efficient economy); this is representative of the differences in MSP of oil-exporting countries from industrial and developing countries. Individual interpretation by country is more important to eliminate the influence of additional factors causing the greater dispersion of ratios than within the individual groups of economies, classified by institutional structure and economic development level, which might represent groups of countries with a specific set of characteristics or similarities in comparison with characteristics and similarities of countries involved in other groups of countries classified in this way.

STRUCTURAL COMPARATIVE ANALYSIS

The comparative structural analysis was designed to test the hypothesis on the role of institutional economic systems, economic development levels, and exogenous sources of influence on the MSP, and to define general conclusions in this respect. It has investigated the creation of the reserve money structure, monetary multipliers, and their relevant ratios (founded on the basic equation of the MSP, $M = {}_cA \cdot m$) in different types of economies through (1) the comparative size of these variables, (2) their ratios, (3) their changes and dispersion in the period under consideration, and (4) determinants of comparative size and of changes and dispersion of these variables and their ratios. We present first the results of the static analysis of the MSP at the end of 1983, followed by conclusions related to changes in the creation of reserve money structure, in monetary multipliers, and in their ratios compared with the end of 1978. Then the conclusions of a dynamic analysis of the MSP (1979–83) are presented to offer an explanation of changes in MSP during this period. Finally, conclusions about the role of institutional sectors and balance-of-payments in MSP, and about control over the MSP, are presented.

Structural Comparative Analysis of the MSP: Late 1983

Monetary multipliers prove the hypothesis that they should be greater in economies at a higher level of economic development. However, in a holistic analysis, the level of economic development influences the MSP indirectly through low differentiation and efficiency in the financial structure of an economy. Therefore, only two significantly different levels of differentiation and efficiency in the financial structure appear in these economies: (1) industrial countries, and (2) developing countries at lower levels. Consequently, empirical evidence reveals much higher monetary multipliers in industrial countries than in other groups of countries, although differences in the size of monetary multipliers within developing economies do not correspond to the rule of a higher monetary multiplier at a higher level of economic development. Contrary to this rule, a lower level of economic development within developing economies is accompanied by a slightly higher monetary multiplier, which reflects the similarities of a less differentiated and efficient financial structure in these economies, and the ramifications of exogenous influences contrary to the rule of decreasing monetary multipliers following a decreasing economic development level.

Empirical evidence proves the hypothesis that monetary multipliers in socialist decentralized economies should be higher than those in capitalist economies at a similar level of economic development. Empirical evidence is also consistent with the hypothesis that monetary multipliers in socialist centralized economies should be lower than in socialist decentralized and capitalist economies at a similar level of economic development. The consistency of the hypotheses with the empirical evidence is proved again by the complex (basic and explanatory) ratios to determine the monetary multiplier.

Empirical evidence shows that ratio p, representing entropy and leakage of reserve money, is the main determinant of the relative size of monetary multipliers by economic system and economic development level. This ratio is far lower in industrial than in other types of economies. Ratio p follows the hypothesis that it should be lower at a higher level of economic development, accompanied by a more efficient financial structure, because of (1) a logically expected lower entropy of reserve money (e), (2) lower holding of currency by nonmonetary entities (c), and (3) lower deposits by nonmonetary entities with the central banking system ($d + {}_ct$). With the influence of the institutional economic systems, it is logical that there is no fundamental difference between capitalist and socialist developing economies, with some variations in entropy and leakage of reserve money. However, it is logical to have a significantly greater ratio p in socialist centralized countries from large holdings of deposits by nonmonetary entities with the central banking system in mainly socialist enterprises, which partly compensates for a lower holding of currency by these entities, e.g., households. (Socialist enterprises are forbidden to hold currency for use in interpayments.)

Reflecting leakage of money in nonmonetary deposits (t) and the monetary effects of foreign exchange transactions (f) or $k = 1 - t + f$, ratio k proves to be capable of modifying the impact of monetary multipliers, as performed by ratio p. Within this framework, ratio k is the dominant influence on the monetary multiplier, moving in an opposite direction from ratio p—consistent with the hypothesis. The lowest ratio k is observed in industrial countries as a logical flow from the highest leakage of money to nonmonetary deposits by monetary institutions (t); creation of money partly compensates for this through the foreign exchange transactions of monetary institutions (f). This ratio k in developing economies is greater because of the lower leakage of money into nonmonetary deposits, partially compensated for by leakage of money through the foreign exchange transactions of monetary institutions.

Ratio k was slightly greater in socialist decentralized economies than in capitalist economies at the same level of economic development because of (1) a lower leakage of money into nonmonetary deposits and (2) compensation for greater leakage of money by the foreign exchange transactions of monetary institutions. A lower ratio k in socialist centralized economies than in socialist decentralized economies revealed a greater leakage of money (ratio t).

The MSP in developing oil-exporting countries reflects the more diverse influences at the lower level of economic development than is found in industrial countries with the accompanying lower differentiation in financial organization and similarities in surplus balance-of-payments current accounts. Similar to developing capitalist economies, the relatively low monetary multiplier is consistent with low differentiation in the financial organization, while the high leakage of money (ratio k) and very high leakage and entropy of reserve money (ratio p) reflect the influence of a positive balance-of-payments current account and related central government transactions.

Empirical evidence on the creation of reserve money proves the hypothesis on the influence of the institutional system and economic development level on instruments for the creation of reserve money, and the hypothesis on the impact of a deterioration in foreign markets and balance of payments in developing economies. The influence of the economic development level is observed in the role of foreign exchange transactions in reserve money creation because they represent the source for reserve money creation in industrial countries, which is nearly equal to domestic instruments in creation of money. In developing economies, which are more sensitive to the deterioration in foreign markets and the greater influence of a deterioration in balance of payments on the MSP, these instruments represent the instrument for the withdrawal of reserve money. Oil-exporting developing economies are in a specific category with foreign exchange transactions as the greater source for reserve money creation than industrial countries, a result of the large surplus of current account balance-of-payments transactions.

The influence of economic systems is reflected in the creation of reserve money by domestic instruments in economies with decentralized economic decisionmaking (capitalist and socialist) and the different structure of these instruments in socialist centralized economies. Thus, reserve money creation by central bank crediting of the central government represents the main domestic instrument for reserve money creation in all decentralized economies at all levels of economic development. Central bank crediting of other monetary institutions is the second most important for reserve money creation. The influence of the economic development level is defined only in terms of the role extraordinary central bank interventions play as sources for reserve money creation. This ranks as the third most important source for the creation of this money in developing capitalist economies because of their (1) sensitivity to deteriorating foreign markets, (2) deteriorating balance of payments, and (3) influence on domestic economic developments. The authority of the economic system over the creation of reserve money operates within a different structure in socialist centralized economies, where the central bank credits to nonmonetary units are the main instrument for reserve money creation.

Comparison of the MSP: Late 1983 and Late 1978

The relative size of monetary multipliers by groups of economies in their classification by institutional economic system and economic development level appears mainly unchanged to reflect the same basic influences of the economic system and level of economic development (late 1978 and late 1983). This is observed despite the different changes in monetary multipliers by groups of economies through different rates of decrease in the multipliers in all groups of economies, except in socialist decentralized economies where there is an increase in monetary multipliers.

The relative size of monetary multipliers by groups of economies has remained stable despite significant changes in leakage of money (ratio k) and leakage/entropy of reserve money (ratio p) through greater rates of decrease in ratio k than in ratio p, contributing to the decrease in monetary multipliers in nearly all groups of economies under study. Comparing these ratios at the end of 1983 with those at the end of 1978, a decrease in ratio p in capitalist economies reflects (1) more rational behavior by monetary institutions in holding reserve money in their accounts with the central banking system (ratio e) under restrictive monetary policy conditions, and (2) reduced demand for currency by nonmonetary entities in the economic development process. In socialist decentralized economies, a decrease in ratio p mainly reflects a decrease in deposits held by nonmonetary entities with the central banking system. Entropy of reserve money (ratio e) was increased to indicate less sensitivity by monetary institutions in these economies to the costs of holding reserve money with the central banking system, and the effects of restrictive monetary policy measures, including an increase in the reserve requirements rate. More of a decrease occurred in leakage of money (ratio k) than in ratio p, which mainly reflects the effects of deterioration in balance of payments in developing economies and less money creation by foreign exchange transactions in developed economies.

By comparison, the creation of reserve money (late 1983) appears significantly different from data at the end of 1978. The basic change in the foreign exchange transactions by central banks was accompanied by significant modifications to the reserve money structure by domestic instruments. The most dramatic change occurred in the foreign exchange transactions by central banks on reserve money creation through (1) withdrawal of reserve money by these transactions in capitalist developing economies, instead of creating this money (end 1978); (2) greater withdrawal of this money by foreign exchange transactions in socialist decentralized economies from deteriorating balance of payments; (3) greater creation of reserve money by oil-exporting countries as a reflection of the surplus of balance-of-payments account; (4) decrease in withdrawal of reserve money in socialist centralized countries that reflect regulations; and (5) no significant change in industrial countries.

The most pronounced changes in the creation of reserve money by domestic instruments came through the increased share of reserve money creation by extraordinary central bank interventions under deteriorating economic developments. Central bank credits to the central government have remained the main source for reserve money creation by domestic instruments; however, their share in reserve money creation has significantly increased in capitalist developing economies and socialist decentralized economies to replace the disappearance or decrease in reserve money creation by foreign exchange transactions. No significant change is observable in industrial countries and socialist centralized economies registering no change in their participation in foreign exchange transactions as a source for reserve money creation.

Dynamic Approach to an Analysis of the MSP: 1979–83

In the flows of 1979–83, the flow monetary multipliers, their ratios, and reserve money creation offer an explanation of changes in the stock approach. These changes are more widespread and dispersed than in a stock approach but not less consistent with the hypothesis on the function of (1) institutional economic systems, (2) levels of economic development, and (3) the role of exogenous influences on the MSP. The additional contribution of this flow approach analysis of the MSP comes from a closer relationship to current economic developments and changes in economic developments related to balance-of-payments transactions.

The lower monetary multipliers in capitalist economies and socialist centralized economies explain the decrease in their stock multipliers while the higher monetary multiplier in socialist decentralized economies explains the increase in their stock monetary multiplier. The greater flow multiplier of oil-exporting countries is not consistent with the reduced stock multiplier caused by a strong asymmetry in dispersion of these multipliers.

The relative size of flow monetary multipliers by groups of economies also explains the unchanged relative size of these multipliers at the end of 1983, compared with the end of 1978. Two exceptions surface: (1) the extra high monetary multiplier of socialist decentralized economies appears greater than that of industrial countries; and (2) the rule of increasing monetary multipliers following a decreasing economic development level within developing economies (late 1978) is not followed in flow monetary multipliers.

Similar to stock monetary multipliers, the relative size of these multipliers by groups of economies has primarily been determined by the relative size of leakage and entropy of reserve money (ratio p)—greater in economies at a lower level of economic development. A similar effect is observed in leakage of money (ratio k) in the relative size of monetary multipliers in stock multipliers. This modifies the impact of leakage and entropy of reserve money (ratio p) on the relative size of monetary multipliers by groups of economies, without changing the basic relationships of these monetary multipliers by groups of economies, e.g., stock multipliers. Leakage of money (ratio k) has had a strong impact on changes in the size of monetary multipliers in comparison with stock multipliers (late 1978) in exposure to the stronger influence of a deterioration in balance of payments than leakage and entropy of reserve money (ratio p), particularly in developing economies.

The creation of reserve money was strongly influenced by a deterioration in balance-of-payments transactions in developing economies, which is reflected in the transformation of foreign exchange transactions as a source for reserve money creation into instruments for the (1) withdrawal of reserve money in capitalist developing economies, excluding oil-exporting countries, and (2) increased withdrawal of reserve money by these transactions in socialist economies. This contributed to changes in the creation of reserve money at the end of 1983 compared with the end of 1978.

Within domestic instruments for reserve money creation, the main change compared with the end of 1978 has been an increased share of extraordinary financing by central banks ($_cU_a$), which reflects an increased need for this type of financing in developing economies (capitalist and socialist) in a climate of deteriorating balance-of-payments transactions and related domestic economic developments. This explains the changes in the creation of reserve money in static consideration (late 1983 in comparison with late 1978).

The dynamic approach analysis of the MSP explains changes in stock monetary multipliers, their ratios, and the reserve money creation structure (late 1978 to late 1983). It is also consistent with the hypothesis on the role of the institutional economic system, economic development level on the MSP, and the hypothesis on modifications to their role by exogenous influences from a significant deterioration in foreign markets and balance of payments, as proved by the static approach analysis of the MSP. The significant characteristic of dynamic monetary multipliers, their ratios, and creation of reserve money is their greater dispersion in comparison with static multipliers, ratios, and reserve money creation structure, with their accompanying greater changes overriding the static approach.

CONCLUSIONS RELEVANT TO MONETARY THEORY AND POLICY

The creation of money represents one of the four basic interrelated questions about monetary theory, with monetary aggregates, demand for money, and the monetary equilibrium process. It is logical to assume that a comparative analysis of the MSP may contribute to a reinvestigation and readjustment of traditional concepts and views about monetary theory, the MSP, and other related questions. Comparative analysis findings about the MSP contribute to a greater generality of concepts and conclusions about existing monetary theory—mainly related to capitalist economies at the highest level of economic development. Two contributions to a comparative analysis of the MSP and monetary theory prove to be the most significant: (1) an explanation of the relative nature of the MSP and monetary processes, as they relate to institutional economic system influences and economic development level; and (2) an explanation of differences in the role of nonmonetary institutional sectors in the MSP (domestic and foreign), with the MSP as part of a broader monetary picture representing the different environments relevant to it in these different types of economies.

The analysis of the relative nature of the MSP and other monetary processes can contribute to the realization that some variables and relationships are neglected in existing monetary theories. The interpretation of some variables and ratios is oversimplified, assuming conditions existing only in a relatively small number of economies at the highest level of economic development, with the monetary and financial organization at the highest level of differentiation and efficiency. Comparative analysis findings about the MSP contribute to more generalization about monetary theory in the differentiation of economies, institutional economic systems, and economic development levels, as the structure of relevant variables and their rules about their interrelationships to the differentiated economic structure of today are adjusted. This may cause a readjustment of the existing equations about the MSP that would include variables, ratios, and parameters reflecting the influence of the institutional economic system and economic development level.

In an illustration of this approach, two equations about monetary multipliers in two types of institutional economic systems can be presented: one with the highest degree of decentralization and the second with the lowest degree of decentralization and economic decisionmaking freedom. Thus

$$m = (1 - t + f) : (e + c + d + ct)$$

represents the monetary multiplier in economies with decentralized economic decisionmaking, and

$$m = 1 - t$$

represents the monetary multiplier in orthodox socialist economies with centralized economic decisionmaking.

Differentiation in the static and dynamic approach to an analysis of the MSP and relationships between variables used in these two approaches contribute to greater generality in the conclusions about monetary theory in the MSP.

A specific contribution of comparative analysis of the MSP to monetary theory comes from the analysis of the influence of institutional sectors based on the hypothesis that not only monetary but also nonmonetary institutional sectors significantly influence the MSP. This approach and the findings of a comparative analysis of the MSP raise two points: (1) the relationship of this approach to the MSP—the monetary theory view that "money matters," and (2) how monetary authorities are able to control the quantity of money. The apparent contradiction between the idea that nonmonetary sectors are able to influence the MSP, i.e., quantity of money, and the predominant view that money matters and monetary authorities are able to control the quantity of money, is explored and resolved in the conclusion of this comparative analysis of the MSP.

Monetary authorities are able to control the maximal quantity of money, while other monetary institutions are able to decide on the total or partial use of this maximal level of money created or the use of the maximal level of their investments as determined by monetary authorities/control measures. In addition, the nonmonetary institutional sectors can decide to use all or part of the maximal level of creation of money, as decided by other monetary institutions, or the total or a part of the supply of their credits. The closer the maximal level of money creation, as decided by monetary authorities, to a level matching the decision made by other monetary authorities and the needs (demand) of nonmonetary entities, the more efficient and realistic is control over the quantity of money by monetary authorities. These factors accompany the rule that monetary authorities are able to control the quantity of money by a "money matters" approach, parallel with the rule that other monetary institutions and nonmonetary entities can influence the MSP.

Comparative analysis of relevant variables and the role of institutional sectors can also contribute to more general monetary theory conclusions. Institutional sectors and their behavior in demand for money and money holding also deserve attention. Behavioral patterns in different institutional sectors and economic systems involve different motivations for size of demand for money, different degrees of exactness of their assessment of appropriate demand for money, and their sensitivity to deviations in the quantity of money held by economic subjects in different institutional sectors from their assessment of the quantity of money corresponding to their demand for money, i.e., the degree and time lag in relation to elimination of extra money holdings. As a rule, it is found in the behavior of governments in all economic systems and socialist enterprises in socialist economies that they represent residual sectors, with low or no sensitivity to holdings of extra quantities of money—important to monetary theory and monetary policy considerations.

The significant contribution of a comparative analysis of the MSP to a greater generality of monetary theory and financial theory may be expected from considering the MSP as a part of the broader monetary process, e.g., monetary equilibrium process, involving monetary and financial/nonfinancial transactions. Thus, this broader approach to comparative analysis of the MSP may be considered a part of a comparative analysis of the broader structure of financial behavior or comparative analysis of the "utility maximization" portfolio selection behavior of economic units in demand for money and for other financial/nonfinancial assets as part of the MSP. In this respect, a comparative analysis of the behavior of nonmonetary entities in (1) holding nonmonetary deposits and other nonmonetary instruments issued by other monetary institutions, (2) holding foreign exchange assets or involvement in foreign exchange liabilities, (3) holding currency in circulation, and (4) holding monetary and nonmonetary deposits with the central banking system may capture the interest of monetary and financial theory. Within this framework, comparative analysis relationships between the MSP, demand for money, and demand for other financial/nonfinancial assets as a counterpart to demand-for-money merit attention in direct and indirect relationships in the monetary equilibrium process. This approach to a comparative analysis of the MSP specifically reflects (1) the appropriate classification of relevant variables and their ratios (basic ratios t, f, c, d, ct; explanatory ratios tq, tu, fa, fi, ctq, ctu; and (2) classification of these ratios to ratios on leakage of money/reserve money and entropy of reserve money relating to their involvement in the MSP in other monetary processes and a broader portfolio selection behavior of nonmonetary entities. Comparative analysis of the MSP and an analysis of these ratios in different economies, with different institutional economic systems and levels of economic development, represent a comparative analysis of the broader monetary and other financial processes that contribute to a greater generality of monetary theory and other financial theories to stimulate greater generalities in investigations and conclusions about these theories.

In related monetary theory–monetary policy relationships, the contributions of a comparative analysis of the MSP to monetary theory offers also a contribution to monetary policy in respect to monetary planning and the implementation of planned targets. The findings of a comparative analysis of the MSP on the relative nature of the monetary processes reflect (1) the relative nature of monetary policy goals, targets, and instruments; (2) the role of variables and ratios in the monetary processes and the influence of exogenous factors on these processes; and (3) stability of relevant ratios and degree of their controllability in economies with different institutional economic systems and varying levels of economic development.

The findings of comparative analysis of the MSP may be especially significant for monetary authorities in developing economies. These findings may provide monetary authorities in these economies with a better understanding of the possibilities and preconditions for an appropriate use of the experiences gleaned from monetary policy experience in developed economies in monetary planning, implementation of planned targets, and the use of monetary instruments for this purpose. The findings of a comparative analysis of the MSP may be expected to contribute to a better understanding of the need for (1) the appropriate structure of institutional changes, (2) adjustments in monetary policy instruments, and (3) monetary policy methods of control over monetary development. The findings of a comparative analysis of the MSP may prove useful particularly in cases of strong exogenous influences on monetary processes from deteriorating foreign markets and balance of payments influencing the monetary processes and economic developments especially in developing economies.

CONCLUSIONS RELEVANT TO INTERNATIONAL FINANCING

The concept of comparative analysis in countries with different levels of economic development and institutional economic systems suggests that its findings are relevant to international financing. The increased interdependence of economies reflects the widespread foreign indebtedness of developing economies and their need to borrow from developed economies. Comparative analysis of the MSP, as discussed in this study, may significantly contribute to a better understanding between lenders and borrowers in international financing. Under these conditions, a better understanding between lenders and borrowers at different levels of economic development and with different economic systems in a context of "conditionality" (proof of creditworthiness of developing economies) can help to avoid mistakes that may have unpredictable and unwanted negative consequences.[1]

Mistakes may occur within the framework of the foreign indebtedness of developing economies. They are more likely if the financial organization in these developing economies is not properly understood and if the rules, assumed to be valid for developed economies, are rigidly applied. The negative effect may be an excessively restrictive economic policy, especially in restrictive monetary policy measures, which may lead to a slowdown in economic growth and production and a decline in possibilities for regular foreign debt servicing. A better understanding of the economic climate in developing economies along with their financial organization may contribute to finding an optimal solution for economic policy measures to promote economic growth.

Conclusions on a comparative analysis of the MSP may in this way appear significant for lenders in developed economies and for their assessment and support of the creditworthiness of borrowers in developing economies.

Comparative analysis of the MSP shows that in developing economies, the MSP is more involved in the financial processes than in developed economies, where there is greater differentiation in financial institutions (nonmonetary institutions and financial markets). In developing economies monetary institutions are at the center of the financial organization, so that transactions in the MSP play a dominant role in total financial transactions. Consequently, measures designed to control the MSP simultaneously control most of the financial transactions, which is very important in the case of restrictive monetary policy measures, which are more indigenous to developing economies than to developed economies in slowing down financing, investments, and production. In addition, the comparative analysis of the MSP shows that monetary multipliers are lower in developing economies than in developed economies because of a greater leakage and entropy of reserve money (ratio p). This means that in developing economies, the same increase in money supply

requires a greater creation of reserve money than in developed economies. The same is valid for an increase in bank credits; the same amount
of bank credit for developing economies requires a greater amount of
reserve money than for developed economies.

There is, however, a lower leakage of money in the nonmonetary
liabilities of monetary institutions (ratio t) in developing countries so that
bank credit amounts in developing economies result in greater money
supply than in developed economies.

Then, there is a greater sensitivity in developing economies to the
deterioration in foreign markets, which results in deterioration of balance
of payments and wider involvement by monetary institutions in foreign
financing, as reflected in the withdrawal of money and reserve money
by foreign exchange transactions by monetary institutions. This means
that foreign exchange transactions in developing economies have a
stronger influence on leakage of money—contrary to lower leakage of
money in nonmonetary deposits—and leakage of reserve money. This is
an important point to be considered in defining the "conditionality"
requirements of developing economies. If "conditionality" requirements
include a sharp improvement in the balance-of-payments current account—a surplus, instead of the traditional deficit in this account—this
will result in the creation, instead of the traditional leakage, of money
and reserve money by foreign exchange transactions by monetary
institutions in these economies. This means that a restrictive monetary
policy is imposed in that case to compensate for the new source of money
creation and reserve money, by foreign exchange transactions leading to
(1) restrictive financing of investments, (2) decrease in production and
employment, and (3) slowing down of economic growth. These factors
serve to decrease the debt servicing potential of developing economies
and their creditworthiness.

A wide range of differences in the relevant relationships of individual
economies at the same level of economic development and in their
sensitivity to exogenous influences suggests that each developing economy may have its own individual set of characteristics. Therefore, the
above conclusions should serve to stimulate an investigation of the
conditions in individual developing economies rather than to promote
conclusions valid for all developing economies.

A comparative analysis of the MSP in socialist centralized and socialist
decentralized economies presents relevant characteristics to international
financing that should be received with tolerance. Unfortunately, there is
often a dogmatic application of rules and assumptions more suitable for

developed capitalist economies than capitalist developing economies and socialist economies.

NOTE

1. The results of monetary and financial policy mistakes are suggested in the American experience during the Great Depression by Milton Friedman and Anna J. Schwartz in *A Monetary History of the United States 1867–1960* (Princeton, NJ: Princeton University Press, 1963).

Bibliography

Bhattacharya, B. B. "Demand and Supply of Money in a Developing Economy: A Structural Analysis for India." *Review of Economics and Statistics* 56 (1974).

Brunner, Karl. "A Schema for the Supply Theory of Money." *International Economic Review* (January 1961).

_____. "The Structure of the Monetary System and the Supply Function of Money." Unpublished paper (1961).

_____. "Some Further Investigations of Demand and Supply Functions of Money." *Journal of Finance* 19 (May 1964).

Brunner, Karl, and Allan Meltzer. "Predicting Velocity: Implications for Theory and Policy." *Journal of Finance* 18 (May 1963).

Burger, Albert E. *The Money Supply Process*. Belmont, CA: Wadsworth, 1971.

Cagan, Phillip. *Determinants and Effects of Changes in the Stock of Money, 1875–1960*. New York: Columbia University Press, 1965.

Dimitrijevic, Dimitrije. "The Financial Structure in a Changing Economy: The Case of Yugoslavia." *Florida State University Slavic Papers*. Vol. 2 (1968).

_____. "The Use of Flow of Funds Accounts in Monetary Planning in Yugoslavia." *Review of Income and Wealth. Journal of International Association for Research in Income and Wealth* 1 (1969).

_____. "Determinants of the Money Supply in Yugoslavia." *Kredit und Capital*. Proceedings of the First Konstanzer Seminar in Monetary Theory and Policy. Berlin: Duncker und Humbolt, 1972.

_____. *Monetarna analiza*. Nish: Institut Edvard Kardelj, 1981.

Dimitrijevic, Dimitrije, and George Macesich. *Money and Finance in Contemporary Yugoslavia*. New York: Praeger, 1973.

Dimitrijevic, Dimitrije, George Macesich, and J. S. Dusenberry. "The Portfolio Approach to the Demand for Money and Other Assets." *Review of Economics and Statistics*. Supplement (February 1963).

Fand, David. "Some Implications of Money Supply Analysis." *Papers and Proceedings of the American Economic Association* 57 (May 1967).

Federal Reserve Bank of St. Louis. "The Three Approaches to Money Stock Analysis." Working Paper No. 1. (1967).
_____. "A Summary of the Brunner-Meltzer Non-Linear Money Supply Hypothesis." Working Paper No. 7. (1968).
Friedman, Milton. "The Demand for Money—Some Theoretical and Empirical Results." *Journal of Political Economy* 67 (June 1959).
_____. "A Theoretical Framework for Monetary Analysis." *Journal of Political Economy* 78 (April-May 1970).
Friedman, Milton, and Anna J. Schwartz. *A Monetary History of the United States 1867–1960.* Princeton, NJ: Princeton University Press, 1963.
Georgescu-Roegen, Nicholas. *Analytical Economics.* Cambridge, MA: Harvard University Press, 1966.
_____. *The Entropy Law and Economic Process.* Cambridge, MA: Harvard University Press, 1971.
Goldsmith, Raymond W. *Financial Structure and Development.* New Haven, CT: Yale University Press, 1969.
Gruchy, A. G. *Comparative Economic Systems,* 2nd ed. Boston: Houghton Mifflin, 1977.
Hamburger, M. J. "The Demand for Money by Households, Money Substitutes, and Monetary Policy." *Journal of Political Economy* 74 (December 1966).
Hart, Albert G. "Commentary." In *Issues in Banking and Monetary Analysis,* edited by G. Pontecorvo, R. P. Shay, and A. G. Hart. New York: Holt, Rinehart, and Winston, 1967.
Haulman, Clyde Austin. "Determinants of the Money Supply in Canada, 1875–1964." Ph.D. diss., Florida State University (1969).
Hendershoot, P. H., and F. De Leeuw. "Free Reserves, Interest Rates and Deposits: A Synthesis." *Journal of Finance* (May 1957).
Holbik, Karel, ed. *Monetary Policy in Twelve Industrial Countries.* Boston: Federal Reserve Bank of Boston, 1973.
Horwich, George. "Elements of Timing and Response in the Balance Sheet of Banking, 1953–55." *Journal of Finance* (May 1957).
International Monetary Fund. *International Financial Statistics.* Washington, DC, 1984.
_____. "A Guide to Money and Banking Statistics." In *International Financial Statistics* (1984).
_____. "Report on the World Current Account Discrepancy." (1987).
Johnson, H. G. "Monetary Theory and Policy." *American Economic Review* (June 1962).
Kenen, Peter P. "Toward a Supranational Monetary System." In *Issues in Banking and Monetary Analysis,* G. Pontecorvo, R. P. Shay, and A. G. Hart, eds. New York: Holt, Rinehart, and Winston, 1967.
Laidler, David E. *The Demand for Money: Theories and Evidence.* Scranton, PA: International Textbook Co., 1969.
Lakatos, Imre. *The Methodology of Scientific Research Programs and Mathematics, Science and Epistemology.* New York: Cambridge University Press, 1978.
Latane, H. A. "Cash Balances and the Interest Rate—A Pragmatic Approach." *Review of Economics and Statistics* (November 1954).
Liu, Fu-Chi. *Essays on Monetary Development in Taiwan.* Taipei: China Committee for Publication Aid and Prize Awards, 1970.

Macesich, George. "The Theory of Economic Integration and the Experience of the Balkan and Danubian Countries before 1914." Paper delivered before the First International Congress on Southeast European Studies, Sofia, Bulgaria (August-September 1966). *Florida State University Slavic Papers*. Vol. 3 (1969).

_____. "Monetary Velocity and Investment Multiplier Stability Relativity for Norway and Sweden." *Statsoknonmisk and Tidsskrift*, 1969.

_____. "Supply and Demand for Money in Canada." In *Varieties of Monetary Experience*, David Meiselman, ed. Chicago: University of Chicago Press, 1970.

_____. *Money in a European Common Market Setting*. Baden-Baden: Nomos Verlagsgesellschaft, 1972.

_____. *The International Monetary Economy and the Third World*. New York: Praeger, 1981.

Macesich, George, and F. A. Close. "A Comparative Stability of Monetary Velocity and the Investment Multiplier of Austria and Yugoslavia." *Florida State University Slavic Papers*. Vol. 3 (1969).

Macesich, George, and Hui Liang Tsai. *Money in Economic Systems*. New York: Praeger, 1983.

Meigs, A. J. *Free Reserves and the Money Supply*. Chicago: University of Chicago Press, 1962.

Meltzer, Allan. "The French Money Supply 1938-1954." *Journal of Political Economy* 67 (June 1959).

Minsky, H. P. "Central Banking and Money Market Changes." *Quarterly Journal of Economics* (May 1957).

Modigliani, F., R. H. Rasche, and J. P. Cooper. "Central Bank Policy, the Money Supply and the Short Term of Interest." *Journal of Money, Credit and Banking* 2 (May 1970).

Parkin, N., I. Richards, and G. Zis. "The Determination and Control of the World Money Supply under Fixed Exchange Rates, 1961-71." *The Manchester School* 43 (September 1975).

Polak, J. J., and W. H. White. "The Effects of Income Expansion on the Quality of Money." *IMF Staff Papers* 4 (August 1955).

Schmidt, Wilson E. "Commentary." In *Issues in Banking and Monetary Analysis*, G. Pontecorvo, R. P. Shay, and A. G. Hart, eds. New York: Holt, Rinehart, and Winston, 1967.

Smith, P. E. "Money Supply and Demand: A Cobweb?" *International Economic Review* 8 (February 1967).

Teigen, Ronald L. "Demand and Supply Functions for Money in the United States: Some Structural Estimates." *Econometrica* (October 1964).

Teigen, Ronald L., and W. L. Smith. "The Demand for and Supply of Money." *Readings in Money, National Income, and Stabilization Policy*. Homewood, IL: Irwin, 1965.

U.S. Congress. Joint Economic Committee, 88th Cong., 1st Sess. "Comparative Features of Central Banks in Selected Foreign Countries." Washington, DC: U.S. Government Printing Office, 1963.

World Bank. *Atlas*. Washington, DC.

Index

ABOUT THE AUTHORS

DIMITRIJE DIMITRIJEVIC is Professor of Economics at the University of Skopje. He is formerly the General Manager of the National Bank of Yugoslavia. Among his previous books are *Money in Economic Systems* (Praeger, 1982), and *Money and Finance in Yugoslavia: A Comparative Analysis* (Praeger, 1983).

GEORGE MACESICH is Professor of Economics and Director of the Center for Yugoslav-American Studies, Research, and Exchanges at Florida State University. His previous books include *Monetary Policy and Rational Expectations* (Praeger, 1987), and *Money and Democracy* (Praeger, 1990).